Stars and Strife

Stars and Strife

The Coming Conflicts between the USA and the European Union

John Redwood

palgrave

First published 2001 by
PALGRAVE
Houndmills, Basingstoke, Hampshire RG21 6XS and
175 Fifth Avenue, New York, N. Y. 10010
Companies and representatives throughout the world

PALGRAVE is the new global academic imprint of
St. Martin's Press LLC Scholarly and Reference Division and
Palgrave Publishers Ltd (formerly Macmillan Press Ltd).

ISBN 0–333–91840–1 hardback
ISBN 0–333–91841–X paperback

This book is printed on paper suitable for recycling and
made from fully managed and sustained forest sources.

A catalogue record for this book is available
from the British Library.

Library of Congress Cataloging-in-Publication Data
Redwood, John.
    Stars & strife : the coming conflicts between the USA
and the European Union / John Redwood.
        p. cm.
    Includes bibliographical references and index.
    ISBN 0–333–91840–1 (cloth)
    1. European Union—United States. 2. International
economic integration. I. Title: Stars and strife. II. Title.
    KJE5112.U6 R44 2001
    341.242'2'0973—dc21
                                                    00–069868

10   9   8   7   6   5   4   3   2
10   09 08 07 06 05 04 03 02 01

Printed and bound in Great Britain by
Antony Rowe Ltd, Chippenham, Wiltshire

Contents

Preface

It took me a little while to understand just what modernisation meant to the new Labour government that swept to power in Britain in 1997. It took me an equally long time to think through how the Anglo-American relationship was being subtly but dramatically changed by the Clinton–Blair axis as the twentieth century drew to a close. I started to write my book *The Death of Britain?* setting out the whole array of constitutional and cultural changes that the British government was trying to bring about, to get the UK to fit in more easily and comfortably with the European Union plan.

After it was published, I discovered I was not alone in fearing for the future of the Mother of Parliaments and the style of combative democracy and national unity that had been pioneered in the British islands offshore from Western Europe. I had worried in case my book and its title were too sensational. When I started writing, few thought the very future of our democracy as we know it was in question. By the time I had finished writing, others were coming to the same conclusion.

Shortly after *The Death of Britain?* Peter Hitchens produced his excellent *The Abolition of Britain* (1999) which tackled the same subject and idea from a different vantage point, placing more emphasis on the educational and cultural changes of some thirty years and rather less on the constitutional changes now underway. Simon Heffer wrote his elegant and distinctive *Nor Shall my Sword* (1999), and Andrew Marr, from a centre-left viewpoint, weighed in with *The Day Britain Died* (2000). All of us agreed from our different starting points that the new pressures on Britain are great and could succeed in breaking the country apart.

Many people read one or more of these books, and joined the debate which was underway in the media and the newspapers. Soon it became very apparent that the warnings were well heeded, but people felt the need for something more positive. They kept asking me, 'What is the alternative? What can we do to prevent this chain of events which we, too, fear will happen?' 'Is there any way', they asked, 'that we can be modern and be part of global economic success? What is the alternative to the European destiny which many leaders implicitly accept but fear to voice openly?'

I decided it was time to set out at greater length an idea that I had started off in 1995 when visiting Washington. If freer trade and a common market made sense for the Europeans in Western Europe, and separately made sense for North Americans through NAFTA (the North American Free Trade Agreement), why couldn't Britain bring the two together, or enjoy both? It led me to ask why some US policy-makers thought the creation of a United Europe to be a good idea, when it was likely to be unfriendly to the US, and to create disputes and troubles in trade, foreign policy, environmental policy and defence.

The Conservative government in Britain in 1996 adopted the policy of widening free trade by negotiation between the EU and NAFTA. It was left ambiguous as to whether Britain itself would seek to join if the EU, as a whole, would not. This policy was sharpened and renewed in Opposition in 1998. Republicans in the US have also proposed this, from Speaker Gingrich through to Senator Gramm. It is an idea whose time is coming.

This book is intended to remind the British people that we are part of a huge English-speaking community through the Commonwealth and the special relationship with the US. It alerts US policy-makers to the importance of the changes underway as Europe presses towards Union. It seeks that understanding and common working across the Atlantic between the old English-speaking world and the new, in the belief that democracy, free trade and liberty are the best ways forward for both of us. It warns that the emerging super-state, the United States of Europe, does not share these Anglo-Saxon values.

Introduction

The emergence of a new nation: the United States of Europe

The United States of Europe is going through a painful birth. The emergence of a new, large and potentially powerful nation is going to send shock-waves around the world. The attempt to bring the divergent peoples of Europe together under one government is going to cause strains in Europe. The reverberations will be felt far beyond the shores of the continent.

This book looks at the coming conflicts between the United States of Europe and the Anglo-Saxon world. The tensions with the United Kingdom, a reluctant partner in the wider European project, are obvious and have often been written about. The pending rows with the United States of America are only just becoming apparent to governments and political commentators.

The European way is very different from the Anglo-Saxon way. This book examines both ideas and ideals. There is the English-speaking world's love of liberty, private property, free speech and limited government. Then there is the European belief in bureaucratic solutions, in powerful central government from behind closed doors, managed consensus and banning difficult or 'extreme' views. Europeans think Anglo-Saxon democracy is too individualistic, too free-form, too swashbuckling for good order. Anglo Saxons think European government is too constrained, too regulated, too secretive to be called truly democratic.

I begin by looking at the options available to the United Kingdom. Should we plunge in and become the fifteenth state of Euroland, a leading region in the new United States of Europe? Can we continue to muddle through, half committed but denying that the European project is about creating a new country with a powerful new government? Or should we join the United States of America and other like-minded countries in a wider and more powerful NAFTA?

So many people in the debate today want to present Britain with a take-it-or-leave-it single option. Those who favour the European project claim it is inevitable whilst denying its true objectives. They want us to get on with becoming a region in the new Europe. Some Eurosceptics want us to leave the EU as soon as possible without thinking carefully about what would replace it and how we then go forward. There are in practice at least four possible courses of action for the UK on a spectrum where, at one end, we are much more committed to the European project, and, at the other end, more committed to the English-speaking global markets.

These debates about our future are far from new. Winston Churchill is often quoted, usually out of context. It is true that he wanted a United States of Europe, but he made it equally clear that he did not want the United Kingdom to belong to it. He aimed at a union of the United Kingdom and its Empire and Commonwealth with the United States. Conversely, European thinkers like Chancellor Kohl of Germany drove forward in the belief that Britain, always a reluctant European at best, would be forced to follow after France and Germany and accept the scheme they were designing.

Britain has a very different history from the continental countries. Britain is at peace with its past in a way that many continental countries can never be. Whilst there have been attempts by some British historians to make us feel guilty about the work of our ancestors in China or India by highlighting some of the murkier events of colonial and great-power past, by and large British people are happy that their country has fought on the side of right and liberty in many wars and has often been victorious. We do not have to live down the shame that many French people feel regarding the events of 1940–4. Defeat and collaboration split French communities and led to huge ill-will. We do not have to live in the war's aftermath with the collective guilt that Germany feels about the Holocaust and the aggressive tyranny which Germany offered the European world in the 1940s. We do not wake up every morning like Italians to wonder who might be in government today and which government ministers might be charged with corruption tomorrow.

This means that British people, rightly or wrongly, are not so willing to see their current democracy and governing system snuffed out in the name of European unity.

The third chapter looks at the way the US and the UK have kept their special relationship over the years, and the way they have worked through the United Nations to police the peace and freedom of the world since 1945. Whilst there are some in the US who think the UN and other world bodies are becoming too intrusive, limiting the freedom of action of a democratic country like the US, in practice the UN and other such global bodies leave much more scope for free action to individual countries than the European Union. If a country does not wish to join in a common action by the UN it does not have to. Security Council members like the US and the UK have a veto over action. The wish by the European Union to establish a common army, navy and air force in addition to NATO is a threat to the balance of power which has seen us through the post-1945 world so far.

The fourth chapter examines the ideals of the wider English-speaking Commonwealth and the US. It shows how we share a particular notion of democracy and free trade which is very different from the views of the continental Europeans. The General Agreement on Tariffs and Trade (GATT) has been driven forward by Anglo-Saxon enthusiasm for cutting tariffs and removing other obstacles to free trade. The European Union has been a reluctant partner in these endeavours, usually seeking to protect European industry and agriculture, and expressing considerable reluctance to open the gates to other people's goods and services. The Commonwealth is a quint-essentially Anglo-Saxon type of institution. It does not seek to take wide-ranging powers over the assembled states. It is flexible, freedom-loving and based on common values. It aims to be loose so that countries can use it when they wish, and can adjust to the fast-changing world outside. It is very different from the EU where there is a rule, a Treaty, an iron constitution for everything.

The fifth chapter shows how Britain is going the US way when it comes to tastes, lifestyle and ways of doing business. The internet is a US creation, which is dominated by English-language communica-tion and commercial activity. Europe is struggling to catch up. It is a dot.com world where ideas, services and orders for goods can fly half-way round the world at a touch of a button. The large US corporations are dominant. The UK is an important second force in this world of global commerce, with London the host to one of the world's big three financial markets, and home for more multinational corpora-tions than the other larger European countries. Some see the

European project as an attempt to create a Napoleonic continental system designed to keep the US out. Others realise this is a hopeless task in an age of dematerialised business, where software, computing and media are such important forces for commerce and change.

The book warns the United States of the coming conflicts between the EU and the US. Where the EU is in charge of affairs on the continent there are already substantial rows across the Atlantic. The EU runs agriculture policy for the member states. There are now endless disputes between the EU and the US over levels of subsidy, husbandry techniques and the safety of products. These led to a whole series of trade disputes and bans on each other's products. The EU runs trade policy for European countries. The EU, as a deliberate act of policy, escalates trade disputes with the US, seeking to establish its own position as an important player in trade negotiations and in the day-to-day management of trade relations. Now that the EU is seeking to move into foreign policy and defence we can anticipate a similar deterioration in the relationship in these crucial areas. The European project is born out of a strong anti-Americanism. It will be driven ahead and sustained by the desire to challenge US supremacy in all walks of government life.

In the book I urge US policy-makers to think again about the idea that dialling one number for Europe will make Washington's task easier. I will show how a special alliance with the UK and other like-minded countries around the world is the better option. If the UK is absorbed into the EU fully the separate voice for freedom and free enterprise on the other side of the Atlantic will be silenced. Even a superpower as strong as the US needs moral and political allies that can come out and back it when world opinion is otherwise hostile. It would be a great pity if, having freed the world of so much communist tyranny by winning the battle of ideas, the Anglo Saxons now let the Europeans reassert collectivist vices, high taxes and over-regulation, damaging world trade and prosperity in the process.

Building a stronger NAFTA, leaving the members free to make their own decisions in a democratic way, strengthening the forces of global enterprise, makes sense for the US and the UK. I examine Britain's options, and conclude that Britain, too, will be better served if it remains part of a common market in Western Europe but does not join in the schemes for political and monetary union. It should be quite possible to renegotiate a different deal for Britain, given how fed up the continental countries are with British reluctance to plunge into the whole plan for union.

The two visions: European big government against Anglo-Saxon freedom and democracy

There are two different visions on offer. Some want a protectionist, highly governed Europe which looks after those in work but is no good at getting the unemployed back to work. They want higher taxes because they believe governments spend your money better than you do. They want more rules and regulations because they are suspicious of individual effort and the work of companies in a free enterprise system. They want to shut out people, ideas and capital from other continents because they think this makes it easier to control what is going on. It is a watered-down version of socialist planning, which failed in the 1960s and 1970s, put in a new guise. Instead of government owning everything, it just runs it by proxy through more laws and more taxes.

Others want a free, open, dynamic world where ideas and capital move easily. We want the new technology to be used to strengthen democracy, not to strengthen governments. We want trade to be free, not protected; taxes to be lower, not higher; more attention to be placed on pricing people into jobs, not on excluding them. The UK should be part of the English-speaking NAFTA alliance, a close friend of the United States. There is still another battle to be won if democracy and freedom are to triumph in this world.

A collapsing Britain

There is a crisis of British identity. Those of us born into a settled land thirty or more years ago are shocked that the bedevilling question at the turn of the twenty-first century is, 'Can Britain survive the next couple of decades?' In the 1970s a minority campaign flourished for Scottish and Irish home rule. In 1972 we joined a Common Market with countries on the continent of Europe which developed rapidly into something much more than a free trade area. Today, petty nationalisms and European federalism are uniting to destroy confidence in Britain and Britishness.

Abstruse constitutional debates since 1972 over how we should be governed attracted little interest as politicians argued how to remodel their own jobs and lives. Now the impact of some of their decisions is being felt more widely, as British people slowly wake up to the loss of freedoms. At exactly the same time as the politicians are plunging Britain into a crisis of identity, people themselves are asking the question, 'What does it mean to be British?' A polyglot Britain is in danger of breaking up under the pressures now being exerted upon it.

A nation, like an individual, lives in the present. The present is a strange amalgam of ideas, feelings, half-remembered thoughts from the past, experiences of the present moment and aspirations for the future. We will explore the legacy of the past before casting our mind forward to what might emerge from the pressures now exerted on Britain and the British. We are in a constitutional crisis today. It is now that we have to take our first steps toward solving it. Leaving it for too long will make it more difficult or impossible to sort out.

The impact of the European Union on the UK

So what, then, are the pressures that require understanding and an answer? First is undoubtedly our membership of the European Union. Many people thought we were joining a Common Market when Sir Edward Heath led the country in 1973. That was what they were told by most of the politicians at the time. That idea was given further support when a successful cross-party referendum campaign in 1975 persuaded people that Britain's rightful place was in the Common Market with our European partners. The propaganda of the day assured people that we would still keep our Parliament, our Queen, our law courts, our army, our navy, our currency, our right to independent decision in every field that mattered. We would only need to compromise with our partners on industrial and commercial affairs. People felt this was a price worth paying for the benefits they were promised of greater trade and more prosperity. People could see the advantages of expanding trade with our nearest neighbours on the continent and were prepared to accept the need for some common rules for the conduct of business.

The European Union has journeyed a very long way from the days when it was still possible for British politicians to claim that it was nothing more nor less than a trading club. They knew it was called the

European Economic Community, if one wished to be formal, but preferred the term 'Common Market'. From those early days in the 1970s, most British politicians either did not read or scrupulously ignored the statements in the founding Treaty of Rome in favour of much greater union. It was possible to see in that early treaty the outlines of a European super-state in the making, but most politicians and most electors chose to turn a blind eye to these proposals.

The UK, since 1973, has been gradually losing its innocence about the nature and intentions of our European partners. A succession of decisions and treaties has now persuaded many that the European project is intent upon taking over the individual nations of Europe and welding them into a United States of Europe. Federal, such a state may be. Devolved, some of the power may turn out to be. Nonetheless, the clear outlines of a super-state are there for all to see.

The proto-United States of Europe already has a flag, an anthem, a Parliament, a supreme court, an executive government in the form of the Commission, almost complete control over industrial, commercial and agricultural policy, a growing social policy agenda, the outlines of a common foreign and security policy, a single currency in the making. It wishes to go on from this to have a common army, navy and air force, and reduce still further the areas in which individual nations can impose a veto. It seeks a larger budget to transfer sums of money around the new country, and a stronger presence on the international stage. It is well advanced with its plans for common frontiers, a common definition of citizenship and common immigration policies. It already has something remarkably like a common passport.

It is difficult in the face of all this evidence for people to claim that the intention is other than the creation of a new country. Enthusiasts for this scheme still claim it will be a different kind of country, a looser federation than we are used to in the centralised United Kingdom or even in the fairly centralised Federal Republic of Germany. This point is debatable. It is no longer a matter of debate whether our partners wish to create such a close union. They want to create a new country. The evidence is all around us.

This startling development, which perhaps has only become apparent to a majority of British people within the last couple of years, is a clear threat to the British state and British identity. Whilst national identity is not the same as government identity, the two are strongly connected. It is possible to have a sense of national identity without having a national government, but there are usually tensions if a nation has reached that point. Most of the civil wars and conflicts within states take place when groups within a particular country claim their independence as a separate nation and seek self-government. The Spanish state has found it difficult to contain the Catalan and Basque nations who assert their right to much more independent government. The Canadian state has found it difficult to handle French-speaking Canadians, many of whom feel their French identity is stronger than their loyalty to the federal Canada. British identity is strongly bound up with having a central government based on the Westminster Parliament and the Whitehall machine. It is bound up with the success of Britain as a governing entity over many centuries. It is bound up with Empire, with the safe passage of Empire to Commonwealth, with Britain's role in the wider world and with the way in which Britain in the last couple of centuries has fought on the side of democracy, freedom and self-determination of peoples.

Regionalism in Britain

A second present threat to British identity comes in the strengthening of the regional divisions within the United Kingdom. The United Kingdom only succeeded in uniting the islands of Ireland, Wales, Scotland and England for a relatively brief period in the last thousand years. The successful revolt of the Catholic southern Irish around the time of the First World War ended the union of all the peoples of this island group. The union of what remained has been of much longer provenance, with much deeper roots. The union with Scotland began with the accession of James VI of Scotland to the throne of England as James I in 1603, and was finally cemented in 1707 with the Union of Parliaments. The union with Wales is even older. It was already in existence when Henry Tudor marched on London from the west in 1485. The Tudor kings and queens completed the absorption of the Welsh government system into the English.

Despite the historical roots of the full union, there is no doubt that it is now under stress. Some Ulster Unionists worry that the move towards peace and compromise in Northern Ireland is the beginning of a long process which will see Protestant Northern Ireland absorbed into Catholic southern Ireland as part of an independent republic. It is this worry which has led to a split in the unionist movement and dogged resistance from some sections of unionist opinion. Limited moves towards cross-border government between the two parts of the island of Ireland have worried many unionists. They also fear the reliance on future plebiscites when the balance of Catholic and Protestant may have shifted more in favour of the Catholics.

In Wales, Welsh nationalists can scarcely believe their luck at their success in persuading Westminster to preserve and develop the Welsh cultural heritage. They wish to foment a sense of national grievance and cultural separation. They were successful in persuading previous Conservative governments to introduce compulsory Welsh-language teaching in Welsh schools, recognising that knowledge and mastery of the language was crucial to Welsh nationalist sentiment. Those who want an independent Wales are keen on strengthening the language. Those English-speakers living in the principality who want to remain part of the UK are more worried about this change. More recently, Welsh nationalists have been even more successful with the New Labour government, persuading it to introduce a Welsh Assembly to provide a focus for the Welsh political nation through the elected Assembly representatives. Whilst the Assembly is very much a second-class body compared with the Scottish Parliament, having very limited powers to do anything, and whilst Welsh nationalism is still a minority view, the Welsh nationalists do have their platform and will look forward to future generations of Welsh people knowing rather more Welsh than the preceding ones.

It is in Scotland where the strongest rift in the Union has been made so far. Consistent and tough campaigning by Scottish nationalists has now succeeded in forcing the introduction of a Scottish Parliament. The Parliament has limited tax-raising powers and wide-ranging legislative powers. It has already chosen a number of areas where it is at variance with Westminster. Scottish nationalists are very likely to use the Scottish Parliament as a continuing platform with which to batter the Union. They will seek to identify areas where the Scottish Parliament has no power and claim that it must be given power in the interests of justice and fairness for Edinburgh. The nationalists will look for every opportunity to find policies hammered out in Westminster which they can portray as mean or unfair in Scotland, and seek a different answer through the Edinburgh Parliament. They will place more and more pressure on any governing party in London, especially where the governing party in London is also a governing coalition partner in the Scottish Parliament, as with the current Labour Party.

Global capitalism

At the same time as these strong political pressures are being exerted from Brussels, from Edinburgh, from Cardiff, from Belfast and from Dublin on the once confident and united Kingdom, an avalanche of change is being hurled at the world by the creative and sometimes destructive forces of global capitalism. Whilst these forces hail from Asia and Europe as well as from the US, there is no doubt that in this current phase of capitalist explosion and advance the US is well in the lead and is creating most of the pressures. The world is shrinking by the day; massive strides in telecommunications, computing, television, video and media transmission have created a global marketplace and a sense of global opinion and global news. An event taking place half-way around the world on the streets of Bombay or Manila can be seen instantaneously in New York or London. The internet is proving to be a revolutionary technology. It is overturning traditional ideas of how banking, retail and many other businesses should be conducted. It is linking companies and individuals on a worldwide basis at the touch of a button. Communications have been revolutionised and made much cheaper. Technology is now developing where video and picture can be transmitted instanta-neously via the internet as well as through the broadcast media.

These developments pose new threats to the identity of peoples around the world as the traditional geographical boundaries which help define national identity begin to lose their significance. Mighty US corporations are proving the most successful at creating, developing and using the technology. The twentieth century saw a tidal wave of Americanisation throughout the developed and developing world. As the twenty-first century dawns it is likely that this process will intensify.

The internet age

The internet has exploded into the economic skies like a disintegrat-ing comet. There was enormous expectation as it began its phenomenal rise. Much ink was spilled, many newspaper pages filled with predictions that the internet was going to conquer the globe. For years people have been arguing about how the different technologies of mainframe computers, home computers, telephone wires, facsimile machines, mobile telephones and television would be brought together. Suddenly the answer was there for all to see. The internet brought together film, video, music, home computing, work computing, telecommunications and mobile phones. The internet is a very powerful and dynamic revolutionary technology. It permits long-distance business transactions to take place in an instant. It permits people at home to gain access to the world's greatest libraries of music, film and information. It provides a means for everyone around the world linked to the system to be in minute-by-minute communication with each other and with the large corporations who wish to spread their message and sell their goods and services.

As the twentieth century drew to a close, technological euphoria erupted in the markets of the Western world. The twentieth century had been a triumph for technical and scientific progress. Whilst the century had been deeply scarred by wars and barbarism on a huge scale, it had shown a breathtaking pace of advance when it came to improving everything from transport and the food supply through to weaponry and the equipment of the average home. Some looked back on the twentieth century in amazement and wondered how anything could arrive to cap that. Others more accurately foresaw the quickening of the pace of technological advance. Many of the things that man had been working on as the twentieth century came to its end were so fundamental that they threatened or promised far greater technical change in the new century than had been achieved in the old.

The computing power revolution had been gathering strength for some years. In the 1960s the first generation of large punchcard commercial machines came into use. The colossus was able to perform relatively straightforward arithmetical calculations and to handle substantial data. It had considerably less power than the typical domestic PC today, cost thousands of times more, and took up a huge room in the office building. In the forty or so years that have passed since then we have moved from punchcard to microprocessor, from large to relatively small machines, and we have seen a huge increase in their capabilities. Computing, which was once the prerogative of the larger companies only, is now available to all and sundry at home, at work and even on the move.

What the internet does is to make the global marketplace ever smaller and easier to exploit. It is still very early days for the application of internet technology. People are still learning how to use it. It is more powerful than our ability to manipulate it so far, and it has outrun the commercial ability to exploit it. In the last three years we have been through several phases in the US and British markets in the evaluation of how this new technology will work in practice. There have been two broad camps or schools of thought who have jostled for advantage and supremacy in the press, over the Web, and in the stock markets themselves.

How revolutionary is the internet?

The technological optimists foresee a world in which the internet replaces many older-fashioned ways of doing things. They believe that the global market will come together dramatically, with people and companies offering products and services over the web on a worldwide basis, and in their turn buying from the World Wide Web on a global basis. If someone thinks a car is too expensive in Britain, he or she will visit a website and order one from Belgium. If someone in the US thinks that Paris fashions are better than US-designed wear, he or she will log onto a site and order over the net. Companies will migrate their activities to the lower-wage-cost areas and will hunt the net for the lowest-cost supplier.

The technological revolutionaries believe that whole business areas will be ripped out or destroyed by the growth of the internet. They believe that travel and theatre bookings, music distribution and a great deal of shopping will be carried out online, rather than through specialist businesses operating out of high street premises. They believe that bank branches will close down, building societies will have to join the web or die, insurance brokers and insurance companies will dematerialise, and stockbrokers in physical offices on Wall Street and in the City of London will soon be a thing of the past. So powerful they believe the web to be that they foresee most of us glued to a screen to insure ourselves, to buy our concert tickets, to listen to music, to buy our clothes, to place our weekly grocery order and to trade our shares. Businesses will adapt or die. Some new brands will emerge through exploiting the internet directly; other old-brand companies will adapt and adjust, using the internet as their new and eventually their main, or only, way of offering their product.

Another school of thought sees the internet as a rather more cumbersome addition to a range of selling techniques. They point out that, so far, all those who have set up internet-based brand companies have lost small fortunes or even big ones. No one has yet been able to build a successful cash-generating profitable business on the internet itself starting from scratch. Many have made huge fortunes by setting up loss-making businesses and selling shares in them before disillusion has set in. Some have made fortunes out of supplying the equipment or the internet services to those who are trying to exploit them for commercial uses, but no one has yet succeeded in building a big, national or global brand from nothing using the internet and turning it into a profitable business. This school of thought believes that the expectations of the technological revolutionaries are greatly over-hyped. They see the internet as being rather like mail order in the case of retailing. After a great deal of activity and advertising, mail order has reached a level where around 4 per cent of retail purchases take place by telephone or post rather than in a shop. They foresee the internet displacing some mail order and gaining a very modest market share.

Modern retailers understand that shopping is more than just buying goods or services in the marketplace. For many people, shopping has become a way of life or an important part of their lifestyle. New shopping centres have higher and higher proportions of their space devoted to coffee shops, restaurants, cafés and fast food outlets. The new shopping centre often has a programme of entertainment with a combination of music, street busking and events like book and record launches that mix a commercial purpose with some artistic or cultural input. The high street is fighting back against the challenge of the World Wide Web.

In a strong bull phase up to March 2000, the technological revolutionaries were in the ascendancy in the stock market. Any business which had '.com' or '.co.uk' after its name was immediately accorded a stunning rating. Towards the end of the bull phase cynics were remarking that all you needed to do to be highly prized by the stock market was to have a silly name, lose lots of money, say that you had a strongly developed internet strategy, and your shares would go sky high. If, on the other hand, you had an established brand, a number of physical trading outlets, were still reporting profits and had a more modest view of the impact of the internet on your business, your shares were likely to be marked down and people would be demanding management change. A new mythology grew up about how businesses had to be developed and run.

The internet pioneers decided that traditional names were stuffy, that the world was going to change dramatically as a result of the arrival of the magic screen. When the Prudential decided to enter the internet banking world, it hit upon the name of 'Egg'. Far from being silly it was the very embodiment of all the virtues and vices of the new internet phase. The name 'Egg' was short and therefore easy to type in. It was thoroughly memorable. It gave the Prudential an enormous amount of free publicity, as journalists like writing about things that are easy to link in to good headlines. Everyone clamoured to be the first to use the word 'Egg' in an exciting way in a financial story. Had Pru laid golden eggs? Were the eggs about to be scrambled? Would Pru get egg on its face, or were the eggs it was providing of farmhouse quality and delicious to eat? It was all too easy, and 'Egg' duly achieved instant fame through the combination of a silly but memorable name and a knockout offer.

The second part of internet business success in those heady days lay in providing a much cheaper product than anyone else in the marketplace. 'Egg' aggressively bid for funds by offering a better deposit rate than most others could match. They were soon followed in financial services by people offering credit at lower and lower rates of interest. Amazon.com succeeded in gaining prominence by going into the discounted book market early with a name that was again memorable and different. By offering 25 or 30 per cent off traditional retail prices of books, Amazon soon chalked up substantial sales. It has proved more difficult translating this success into profitability.

The internet theory was based on the assumption that a period of aggressive discounting to establish market share could soon be followed by consolidation and exploitation of the market gains. In order to achieve the rapid growth the analysts hoped for, they also assumed that there would be a frenetic pace of deal-making. Everyone felt that there was no time available to allow the business to grow sedately by organic means. There was not even time to build it suffi-ciently just by aggressive bidding for deposits or book sales by promotional pricing. Anyone who was serious about building an internet business had to think global, think big, and undertake ever-larger deals. The AOL–Time Warner deal was the high watermark of this particular genre. Its architects realised that you needed to marry the content of a Time Warner, an old-fashioned branded business that was making money, with the growth and ambitions of an AOL, an internet service provider that had gained substantial market share by being early and generous in its pricing.

At the end of March 2000 the stock market began to see that all this had become rather absurd. Some of the older virtues that businesses needed to generate cash and profit and pay dividends began to re-emerge in fashion. When the traditional tests for investment were applied to the internet businesses so generously quoted on the stock market, the internet businesses started to collapse.

The telecommunications bubble

Something similar was happening to the valuation of telephone companies. There was more sense in bidding the telephone stocks up because they were building ever more profitable and sizeable businesses out of internet activity. When internet business had first been introduced, people tried to charge for providing the internet service. The telephone companies also charged for the use of the phone line during the time that the link was up and running to the home computer.

In Britain, Dixons decided to launch Freeserve. Dixons was saying that it was scrapping the weekly or monthly charge levied by a traditional internet service provider on its customers. Dixons would provide the linkage free because it had two other ways of rewarding itself. Dixons is a chain of electrical retailers, capable of making money out of selling the original equipment, the computer, the telephone, the modem and the other equipment needed, to the customer. Dixons was also able, through Freeserve, to negotiate a share of the telephone tariff.

During this phase of market development, even though the phone companies were having to share the revenues, the explosion of time spent on the phone lines meant extremely good business for the telephone companies. Concurrently with this new market for traditional telephone links the telephone companies were building up two additional new businesses. Mobile telephones were taking off. Every teenager wanted one for Christmas, every woman felt she had to have one in her handbag in case of trouble, and every businessman knew he had to have one to reschedule his life on the move. Telephone companies charged more for mobile services than for fixed line services and could not believe their luck when, despite the charges, more people bought the phones and spent longer and longer on them. As the phones became lighter and pocket-sized, as parents felt they needed to keep in touch with their teenagers, as traffic jams worsened and people needed to tell the people expecting them how late they were going to be, so mobile telephony went into overdrive.

The combination of greater usage of traditional phone lines, new types of phone line and the mobile telephony revolution led to a huge surge in cashflow, profits and the share prices of the leading telephone companies. Investors who liked a risk or a punt bought the racy internet companies, knowing that there was nothing there, but reckoning that momentum would carry them up further and faster. For a period of months such investors were right. The more cautious investors, who could see that something big was happening, bought into the telephone companies knowing that their shares would be bid up because they would get a slice of the action, but knowing that if the mood changed they would not fall as far or as fast as the pure internet stocks because they continued with a successful, traditional profitable business.

The hi-tech crash of 2000

When the day of reckoning came it was true that the internet stocks fell further and faster than the telephone stocks, but people still had some unpleasant surprises in store from the telephone companies themselves. The wave of price competition, which had hit the original internet service providers when Freeserve made it a market standard to waive all specific charges, continued with others coming into the market offering to cut the price of the phone call element. The telephone companies were now under pressure to share some of their profit margin with the customer as part of the internet drive. At the same time, governments woke up to the enormous sums of money washing around in the telephone companies. Led by the British government, they decided to cash in themselves.

The British government announced that all those telephone companies wishing to use airwave space for their next generation of mobile phones would have to pay a large tax to the British government for the privilege. The auction of the radio spectrum to the mobile phone companies in Britain was watched in amazement and awe from around the world. Early estimates suggested that the companies would pay as much as £5 billion or £6 billion for the privilege of remaining in business and using the airwaves. When the bidding finished at over £22 billion, people were stunned. The companies had decided to give away a huge chunk of their future cashflows and profit before their new networks and new technology had been developed, or were up and running.

Further bad news came with the realisation that new technology would enable the traditional copper wire phone lines into the house to carry much more data and provide a much higher quality service without the need to renew them all with fibre optic or ISDN facilities. Market moods are strange. They often go on for longer than logic would suggest, but when they change, they can change dramatically. The news background, which had all seemed positive for the internet and telephone companies up to March 2000, suddenly looked bleak indeed. The reality was that governments were taking too much of the cash, that customers were not spending enough over the net, and shareholders were at last becoming restless about the lack of profits and dividends.

It is now possible to come to a more balanced view between the competing schools of thought. There is merit in what they both say, but both have exaggerated their case for the sake of a good argument. The internet loosely defined is revolutionary. Bringing together computers, telephones, mobile phones, televisions, databanks, libraries, music, film, video, is going to change the way many things are done. The internet will be an extremely important way of doing business in the years ahead. Few companies now rely upon manual records and manual files. It has taken some twenty years, but most have now converted to using computer systems. No company would think of trying to run its business without a phone line, as it knows how important it is to stay in touch and to have that instant communication which the telephone call or the fax line permits. More and more of this contact will take place through the internet link and e-mail.

The internet will become a powerful means of delivering music, video, entertainment and sport into the home. There will be a coming together of digital TV, satellite TV and internet delivery. The internet means the effective end to two or three channels of television with a take-it-or-leave-it set of options for each evening. The internet will become a strong rival way of delivering all sorts of service products that are already dematerialised, and the internet is a force for making the global market ever more cohesive and truly global.

Brit.com: the internet is English as well as American

The computer revolution and now the internet revolution have been led by the US. In the nineteenth century the United Kingdom first developed a universal postal service. Its reward for being the pioneer was that British postal stamps did not have to carry the name United Kingdom or Great Britain on them, as everyone knew that we were the big leaders in this field. The countries that followed on had to put the names of their countries on their stamps. So it is with the US in the dot.com revolution. Other countries have to put a few letters or symbols of their national identity in their internet address, whereas the United States proudly just puts '.com'.

More importantly, the success of America in developing this technology has meant that it is English-language based. Where the Japanese have been very alert and capable of leading developments in consumer electrical and electronics in areas like handheld games, CD players and radios, the US has taken over in the field of domestic computing and internet communication. Japan might anyway have found it difficult to dominate the World Wide Web using the Japanese language, as it is not nearly as flexible or as universal as the English language, based as it is upon only 26 letters. The library of characters in Japanese or Chinese has posed problems for the makers of intelligent typewriters and home computers which have slowed the whole process down in that part of Asia.

The dominance of English-language products and services is most important for the United Kingdom. The United Kingdom has played a good second string to the US' leading violins and other orchestral instruments. In the story of the coming of the World Wide Web, Freeserve breaking the idea of an internet service provider fee in the UK is an important chapter, and the success of Vodaphone in extending the reach of mobile telephony is also worth a good few paragraphs.

It is this English-language strength which augurs well for the future of the US and her transatlantic ally, the UK.

A stronger global market, led by Anglo-Saxon corporations

The global marketplace was an emerging reality anyway. The large oil companies, the large motorcar manufacturers, the large consumer product companies, had for decades been seeing the world as their oyster. Between 1950 and 1990 there had been rapid progress towards delivering a world product. The number of continental and country variations was gradually reduced, and the amount of global advertising and marketing stepped up. Whereas in the 1960s a US car manufacturer would think of designing a completely different set of products for the US market, for the UK market and separately for the German market, by the 1980s it was thinking of just designing a US range and a European range. By the year 2000 it was designing a global car.

The internet is reinforcing this process. Now that companies wish to compare and contrast prices and specifications of components and raw materials on a worldwide basis, those who wish to serve those marketplaces have to think globally as well. Now that video and film is made available on a worldwide basis, so customers' lifestyle preferences and aspirations start to merge. It is a notable feature of the liberation of Eastern Europe that the first thing people wanted as they emerged from the tyranny of communism was access to the big consumer brands of the West which they had seen or heard about on television or radio and now wished to try for themselves.

Governments have been groping towards regulating a global market as well. Whilst a lot of regulation has been carried out on a nation-by-nation basis, and now there have been further attempts to produce continent-wide regulation, particularly in the European Union area, the real progress that has been made in the last 20 years has occurred through a coming together of the large countries and regions to create a worldwide framework of commercial law and practice.

We will see in other chapters how regulators tackle the growing globalisation of markets. The internet poses enormous difficulties for both national and regional regulation, permitting business to hop across frontiers or evade jurisdiction at the press of a button. Whilst many in the US are understandably wary of a large worldwide regulatory structure, they are also realising that even the US is insufficiently powerful and has insufficient reach to regulate the world of the web on its own. The US and the UK should be powerful voices for less intrusive regulation, but they will need to discuss how much and how with other jurisdictions.

As Britain ponders its future, it would be wise to take into account the phenomenal energies released by internet technology and the impact on the future development of the global economy that the internet is likely to have. The internet is already creating bigger divisions as surely as it makes the world more prosperous and opens up new opportunities. The power offered by internet communications and computing means that some large corporations are now moving their administrative and back office facilities out of the high-wage countries of the West to the lower-wage countries of Asia. It is possible to hire talented, well educated people in a country like India at a fraction of the cost of similarly educated and skilled people in the US, the UK, or continental Europe.

At the same time, the price transparency offered by the internet itself is sharpening further the red pencils of procurement executives in all the large companies. The internet is not causing the pursuit of lowest-cost supply. That was going on long before the internet was invented. The price transparency offered by the internet may not be any greater than the price transparency that can be achieved through the fax and the printed catalogue. However, the internet is being used as an excuse by procurement managers of the large corporations to put further pressure on their suppliers. The internet may also produce new competitors out of the mists of Asia or Latin America who see the opportunity advertised on the website of a major corporation and put in their bid using the e-mail facility. Large corporations always prefer to cut the costs via someone else's business when they buy something rather than cutting out their own overhead directly. Indeed, the justification offered for the high overhead in many large corporations is just that; that they can put incredible pressure on suppliers to get a better deal which will in part be passed on to their final customers in turn.

This means that rich, advanced countries like the United Kingdom have to understand that internet technology is a further pressure in hollowing out the industrial base and in shifting commodity and basic administrative activities away from a high-wage country like Britain to the lower-wage economies of the East. The public policy conclusions from all this are quite obvious. If Britain wishes to maintain and increase its lead in living standards compared with most countries in the world, it has to concentrate on increasing entrepreneurship, better education and raising the skills of the working population. We are going to survive by our wits, not by our brawn. It means that the United Kingdom, if it is to remain competitive, has to keep the costs of government and levels of taxes relatively low. As we wish to pay ourselves good salaries we must not also over-reward our government – to do so would drive us out of the highly competitive markets of the world. We also need to understand the message of internet technology and globalisation for our political relationships.

Some seem to think that if we plunge deeper into the European Union it would somehow protect us from these growing forces of global change and competitive activity. Nothing could be further from the truth. Even the continent is not big enough to hide from these winds of dramatic economic fortune. Europe has to compete and adapt, or die. Europe will not be able to persuade other countries of the world to adopt regulatory and tax levels as high as its own, as it is already very uncompetitive against the US, which remains the world's most powerful country by a long way. The UK would be wise to recognise that we are moving to a world regulatory structure. That regulatory structure is going to be more influenced by the US than by the EU. We can see this already in the way in which GATT and financial regulation worldwide are both moving. Europe would prefer a more protective GATT, is trying to protect agriculture against very strong forces of change, and would like to see a higher tax level than that adopted in America accepted as a worldwide norm as it carries on its crusade against so-called unfair tax competition. The EU is unlikely to win this particular contest.

Given the enormous advantage Britain has by being a bit more flexible than the large countries in the EU, and by sharing the common English language with the US, we have everything to look forward to and to win from the coming internet revolution. British brands can be projected worldwide. British advertising and marketing can be used in this new English-language-dominated medium. British software skills are much in demand, and Britain could produce a budget version of Hollywood and the US music industry to meet the growing demand for good-quality entertainment on a worldwide basis. All this argues in favour of having friendly commercial links with our partners in Europe, but not joining them in their project to create a large, expensive, protective super-state.

If Britain wishes to remain the premier location for inward investment into the European Union, it must have a much more flexible labour market than its near neighbours on the continent. If it adopts all of the protective legislation, making it difficult to sack people and expensive to employ them, it will deter many would-be investors. The continent has discovered that if you protect some of the jobs some of the time too well, you have far fewer jobs overall and many more people out of work than if you adopt the more flexible Anglo-Saxon model. The United Kingdom must understand that it cannot afford the high taxes on the continent if it wishes to earn a good living on a worldwide basis. Britain's taxes are materially below those of France and Germany, and need to stay there to encourage investment and to avoid too large a burden upon domestic entrepreneurs.

The World Wide Web, successive rounds of GATT and the worldwide regulatory framework now emerging under considerable US influence and pressure offers Britain the prospect of a good living in the twenty-first century. We could enjoy this living outside the EU power bloc now being established. It would be extremely difficult to enjoy all the benefits of our potential if we signed up to the single army, the single tax structure, the common economic policy and the common social employment policy which Europe has in mind for its subject countries.

The United States is the mightiest part of an island continent, and the United Kingdom is an island country. People who live on island countries or continents do have different attitudes from those who share the continent cheek by jowl with their neighbours. It makes us both more insular and more outward-looking. For friendship, contact, trade and new ideas we have to look out across the oceans and continents of the world. For government, community and neighbourliness, we look inwards to our own little piece of the earth. The internet and the cultural revolution it inspires will create more of a global community. Through television and video links we will enjoy each other's celebrations and understand more of each other's faiths, outlooks and rituals. This may not make us seek to homogenise and globalise everything.

The paradox of globalisation is that it is intensifying the wish to have local and national roots and to delve back into the past in order to comprehend the future. At exactly the same time that the typical

British family is bracing itself for the world of the web and buying a home computer to enjoy all that is new, the schedules on main television provide a diet of old films, history programmes and programmes about local British communities. At the same time as people want the newest by way of mobile phones and computers, they are queuing up to buy houses built in styles reminiscent of the best of the Elizabethan or Georgian eras. The very same people who want to compare car prices on the web may want to drive that car out to an archaeological site to understand more of where we have come from.

The problem with a project like that to create a United States of Europe is that it is seeking to create something artificial and unnecessary as far as many are concerned, at a time when these conflicting pulls of the new and the global, on the one hand, and the old and the local, on the other, are foremost in people's minds. At a time of great economic and technical change many people want less change rather than more in their government relationship and their community affiliations. There is a great battle going on. The modernisers claim that because the internet and technology are throwing the world of business up into the air it is right for the world of government to be thrown up in the air, and for much government to transfer from our British democracy to the Brussels bureaucracy.

A majority of the British people, a large majority of the British people, take the opposite view. We believe that Britain will survive and thrive by exploiting the English-language-based internet and by being inventive, enterprising, buccaneering and high-spirited. We used to make a good living by trading on the sea, now we will make a better living by trading on the web. At the same time, we wish to remain true to our sense of tradition, custom, civilisation and landscape. We wish to defend the green fields and village greens of Old England. We wish to restore the old manor and maintain the church, even if we are not so keen to worship in it. We wish to revere and understand the past in order to grapple with the future that much more confidently. The United Kingdom is a country many feel proud of. It is not a country time-expired and worn out. We are not ready to consign it to the dustbin of history.

Technology is important but it is not the only thing which will determine our future as a country and as a people. It is time now to look at the four wider political options that present themselves to the UK in this rapidly globalising world.

Our politicians have to understand that the European Union is not suddenly going our way. They have to be honest with the electorate and set out the four possible futures for Britain. It is vital that we choose the world and the web alongside a British democracy, for that is the only way that people will remain happy in these islands. We can combine self-government at home with worldwide commerce abroad. The web is our opportunity. It is a dot.com world. That is something the European Union does not seem to understand. We should be friends with them and trade with them, but we should never turn our backs on the US alliance and the English language. We should be looking to strengthen our ties with the English-speaking world where we will find friendship and much business success. From that base we should go out and offer our services to the new world in the making in Asia which will become dominant.

As we will see later, US influences have been particularly strong on the United Kingdom. British business people are more likely to invest in the US than in foreign-language-speaking France or Germany. Whilst France and Germany are geographically closer, the US business community is so much closer in so many ways that matter – culturally, linguistically, and in sense of purpose. Britain is the largest overseas investor in the US, and the US is the largest overseas investor in Britain. The aspirations of many British people are very American. We can see US influences at work today in our style of retailing, and in the development of computing, telephony and the internet, in our leisure activities and in film and media. If people are looking for a way to entertain their children, their thoughts often turn to Disney. If they are looking for drinks and meals, they may well turn to Coca-Cola and McDonald's. If they are looking for a new home computer and software, they are very likely to buy a US computer and Microsoft packages. The US way of life, with the motor car, the drive-in movie, the T-shirts, jeans and trainers, has arrived in Britain. Many say they like it by living it.

In France, this US invasion matters more. The French feel they are locked in a battle to protect a French identity under pressure from the invasion of US culture. The French state has decided on protecting French cinema and media, giving incentives for the production of French-speaking films to offer some competition to the ubiquitous US movie either dubbed or with sub-titles in a host of foreign languages. The French state has taken to protecting and strengthening the French language, the French metric measurement system, and other symbols of French cultural imperialism. France is pressing on the European Union an agenda of protectionism against certain types of US import, and the development of Euro-champions to offer commercial competition to the US giants at home and abroad. This protectionism extends beyond the cultural world, as the French seek to create a European aviation, media and telecommunications industry.

Britain has not been so worried about this growing Americanisation of life. In recent years there has been a mood of hurrying to adopt and adapt all of the best in US commercial success as a sign of our growing prosperity. Britain has got over its hangdog jealousies of the post-war period when memories of the US army in Britain were still strong and when the sense of British inferiority was transmuted into an attack upon alleged US arrogance and spending power. As the visible gap between US lifestyles and our own has narrowed, so Britons have less to fear from the US invasion. We must turn first to look at the options facing Britain in this fast-changing world, a world so different from the one that confronted the founding fathers of the new Europe in the 1950s when they first pieced together the outlines of a new United Europe.

1
Britain and Britishness at the Crossroads

Today we find Britain and Britishness at a crossroads. Those who feel themselves to be more European in Britain share the French worry about the growing Americanisation of world commercial and cultural life. Those who fear that a European Union will damage those most precious elements of Britishness and British government would rather welcome more commercial influence from the US as a counterweight to European government. It leaves Britain with four possible avenues of development. The choice is close upon us. It will be taken wittingly or unwittingly in the few years that lie ahead.

The four options for Britain

There are four options for Britain to choose from in the next few years. The first is to decide that our destiny does lie with our European partners and to plunge in as a willing partner in the construction of a United States of Europe. We would have to share the French view that the intention of this was to create a mighty counterweight to the power of the United States of America. We would be drawn in to measures and choices which would undoubtedly distance us from our US cousins rather more. The second choice would be to deliberately strengthen our ties with the US as being the best way to enjoy the military protection of US forces and to gain more benefit from the undoubted commercial and technological dynamism of the US peoples. This course of action would include joining the North American Free Trade Agreement (NAFTA) and seeing if that could develop into a wider union of the English-speaking peoples led by the United States with Britain as a strong second force.

The third option is to see if Britain can continue to balance its position as it has tried to do in the last 27 years both by being a member of the EU and by strengthening its trade and friendship links with the United States and the NAFTA. Some people believe it is possible to continue this delicate balancing act, saying no to the more extreme moves towards European federalism, whilst at the same time developing a better relationship with the United States to enjoy defence and commercial collaboration. According to this model we would be in Europe but not run by it. We would remain part of the Common Market but we would refuse to surrender sterling as our currency, and we would have no truck with common defence arrangements. We would have a world role as the United Kingdom, but we would also have influence with our European partners through the institutions of the EU and we would have a special relationship based on common language, common interest and often good working relationships between president and prime minister with the United States.

The fourth option would be to go it alone. There is a gathering body of opinion in Britain which would like to see us pull out of the European Union altogether. Whilst some of those who would like us to pull out argue very strongly for the second option, the English-speaking union based first of all on membership of NAFTA, others believe that Britain is large enough to continue to be an independent country with representation in a number of international fora and trading with the five continents of the world. Those who advocate withdrawal from the European Union advocate negotiating a new set of arrangements so that we could continue to trade on sensible terms with our partners. They point out that companies in the EU member states export more to Britain than British companies export to the continent, so there should be plenty of leverage to get a satisfactory deal. The EU has more to lose than Britain, on this argument, as Britain is a net contributor to the Community budget and as Britain is the importer of last resort for many European countries.

These, then, are the possible courses of action for the United Kingdom. They give the lie to those in the various camps who claim that their future for the UK is the only one available. Many Euro-federalists believe there is no alternative for Britain but to plunge into a proper union with our partners. Many Atlanticists believe there is no hope for Britain unless we do the opposite. Those who believe we can muddle through as we have done in the last 30 years often claim that is the only possible future for Britain. I believe that any one of these futures is possible for Britain. Some of them could work with bold and sensible political leadership.

15th state of Euroland or 51st state of the Union?

It is now time for the politicians and public to debate how each of these futures would be secured and which is the more desirable. It really comes down to defining who we are and what our future should be. It is something where each one of us has to look into our own hearts, minds and memories to ask ourselves, 'How British are we, and how British do we wish to remain?' We could become the 15th state of Euroland. If we do so, we will discover that the main decisions have been taken and many features of the EU structure will not be to our liking. Our size and wealth will make us more than just one 15th partner, but we will not have the weight and influence of Germany or France. We have to accept that the United States of Europe (USE) is an idea fashioned by the Germans and the French, designed as their method of preventing future military conflict between their two countries. We may think such conflict unlikely, or preventable by NATO and other forces. They believe strongly that the structure of the Union is crucial to their futures.

We could try to become the 51st state of the American Union. Many who dislike our drift into European control often propose just such a solution. As I will show, this is more akin to what Churchill had in mind. There would be no language barrier, and less of a legal, cultural and political barrier than submerging ourselves in Europe. It would, however, represent a similar surrender of sovereignty to joining the USE, and be a substantial wrench in a new direction for our foreign policy. It was an option with which Harold Wilson toyed in the 1960s when he was the UK's prime minister.

The first two of these routes offers the abolition or substantial transmutation of Britain and Britishness. It is also quite clear that the fourth requires a substantial strengthening of Britishness which many would claim is now impossible. We must ask ourselves, 'What is Britishness; what are its unique characteristics? Do these unique characteristics make it worthwhile keeping? How British do each of us feel we are, and how British are we likely to feel in the years ahead as the inevitable political, constitutional, economic and personal changes unfold?'

The British character

Britishness is often defined as a set of attitudes developed by the peoples of the United Kingdom in their imperial role. The Empire was quintessentially British. It was purposefully called the British Empire and not the English Empire. It was the plaything of the Scots, the Welsh and the Irish as well as the English. Indeed, it was often the Celtic parts of the United Kingdom that plunged disproportionately into Empire to compensate for some of the problems at home. In the hands of some modern interpretations like Norman Davies' *Europe: A History* (1996), and Andrew Marr's *The Day Britain Died* (1999), the death of Empire is sufficient reason why Britain itself should now die and should be replaced by the English, the Scots, the Welsh and the Irish assuming their more normal and rightful position in European politics.

Britain defined its relationship to Empire through a set of values. Britain exported the English language, the Christian religion, a sense of fair play, honest administration, impartial justice, commercial acumen, industrial enterprise, sporting enthusiasm and military prowess to its conquered territories. In the heyday of empire it is true that Britain was not keen to encourage indigenous manufacture to rival the mighty manufacturing capacity of the home islands. It is true that Britain often introduced no democracy at all when ruling the subject peoples, whilst at the same time developing a red-blooded wide-franchised democracy at home. It is true that a lot of the imperial endeavour was based upon continuous military activity and there were occasions when Britain showed little fairness or tenderness when putting down rebellions or dissent among subject peoples.

It has been fashionable for some years now to write about the darker side of Empire. A group of historians have taken pride in doing Britain down, in highlighting the Black Hole of Calcutta in India, the unpleasant Opium Wars which characterised part of our relationship with China and the concentration camps in the Boer War. It has been less common in recent years to remember the enormous strengths of British imperial achievement and to judge them by the rather barbaric and unpleasant standards of the age in which they were set. Whilst other peoples' and countries' barbarisms cannot excuse any barbarism from the British imperial side, it is important to understand the background, the attitudes and the standards of the day. It is also important to weigh on the scales the undoubted pluses which British Empire brought.

Many British people still see the imperial virtues as characteristics of the British race. The Empire was an expression of Britishness in all senses, not least because the Empire itself was polyglot and Britain itself is now polyglot. The imperial process was a two-way process. Britain took its standards of impartial justice, independent administration and commercial progress to the imperial territories, and received and took back people, artefacts and many aspects of overseas culture from its territories and dominions. We imported the curry, sweet and sour dishes from Asia, tobacco and potatoes from the New World, a feast of food, words and attitudes as British people travelled and learned.

The arrival of a large number of Commonwealth immigrants into Britain in the second half of the twentieth century has brought much of the infinite variety and excitement of Empire back to the home islands. As a result, Britain is now a more tolerant, multiracial and more colourful society. Britishness is the natural identity for dwellers in the home islands wherever they or their parents may have come from.

When a new immigrant settles in London and decides he or she does wish to adopt a new identity that is compatible with his or her new home, it is always British rather than English that they choose. You do not find settlers from Africa or Asia in Edinburgh saying they are Scottish, in London saying they are English, or in Cardiff saying they are Welsh. As they decide to make this their home and adopt a new identity, it is always the British portmanteau identity which they adopt most easily.

The use of words to define who we are is becoming very potent in this new, brittle world of changing identities. If someone now very firmly says to me that he (or she) is English rather than British, I know it probably means that he is tired of paying for the Scots, is becoming keen on the idea of an English Parliament, and is drifting towards a petty English nationalism which would like to tear the Union apart. If a Scot ferociously tells me he is Scottish and not British, I know that he has exactly the same attitudes from north of the border, seeking an independent Scotland as soon as possible, and wishing to turn his back on the old enemy to the south. The word 'British' is now the healing word, the word that tries to bring together, or keep together, divergent peoples of the United Kingdom islands. It will be a much more difficult place for settlers from Eastern Europe, from Asia, from Africa, from the Caribbean, if Britain does fragment into England, Scotland, Wales and Northern Ireland, as those smaller nations will have a more urgent, younger sense of nationhood which is more exclusive than the British idea deliberately created to encompass the world and run an empire.

The rise of nationalist sentiment in the regions of the UK

It is a sense of frustration at the political process which is leading to some fragmentation of political allegiance and loyalty. Whereas in the 1950s and 1960s the Labour and Conservative parties accounted for 85–90 per cent of the vote, today they are lucky to gain 75 per cent of the vote. A quarter of the electorate is now inclined to vote for Welsh Nationalists, Scottish Nationalists, United Kingdom Independence, the Referendum Party and Liberals, as a protest against the two main coalitions. British politics, fractured in the past around the issue of how much government was wanted, with Conservatives offering lower taxes and less government and Labour offering a more enveloping welfare state, now wishes to split over different issues. It is the issues of national and international identity, foreign policy and our relationship with Europe which motivates a significant proportion of the electors who find that the present two-party system does not reflect their passionately held views. This lies behind the disintegration of belief in the British nation and its political expression, the Queen in Parliament.

Tony Blair tells us his Britain is a new country. He seems to think history began in May 1997, when his party swept back into power; or conceivably it began under Margaret Thatcher in the 1980s, an era Blair occasionally conjures up to frighten the children. Anyone who knows Britain better knows that it is an old country. It may have a great future, and we doubtless live in the present, but the past is all around us.

Defining a nation

Some say the past is its own country. Modernisers want to put it behind us, deny it exists, or claim that it is at best an irrelevance and at worst an obstacle to our progress. Yet the past is still our country. It is there in the landscape, in the architecture, in our memories. A country has a past, a present and a future. You can only hope to understand the present and forecast the future if you have first visited the past. You can only work out where we might be going if you know where we have come from.

We each travel daily in our own time machine. Each minute, each second, we decide whether to indulge in memory or spirit-up the future. In our very choice of language we choose a tense for our words. We will make different choices as the day wears on. Each action requires a memory of times past when we did it before.

So it is with a nation. It cannot rid itself of its past, but can in the present draw on those memories of the past which suit it most, or which are most useful to the here and now. A nation can and does change its past by altering perceptions of it. Some nations set out to destroy their ancestry by revolution, rewriting the history books in a wilful act of self-denial. The past usually comes back to haunt them. It lingers on in the landscape and individual memories. A country which tries to destroy its past is not at ease with itself. Our nation has favoured evolution, not revolution; constantly shifting and accommodating the past as each corner of the future opens up a new perspective.

There is a folk memory and a written memory in the form of history. The buildings cannot lie, the landscape changes but slowly, the Church bells toll as they have for centuries, the river winds its way across the lea. Each family remembers exploits great and small, local and national, incidents of huge and of no import, and passes them down from generation to generation.

It happens to each one of us. From the moment we are conceived we have a separate history, but it is one interwoven with the history of our families, our communities, our nation. As we move from home to school so our history shifts from all family to partly local and institutional. Some are more influenced by the past than others. Some are more influenced by national events. Most dwell more in the world of family and local events. A few have a broad and deep knowledge of national history. All have some intuition of our history from their own lives, family anecdotes and half remembered school history.

No-one leads an entirely contemporary life. Some people are self-consciously archaic, others self consciously modern or futuristic. All to some extent live in the past. Everyone owns furniture and personal effects acquired over many years. From the day the new toy is delivered to the child, an ageing process starts for both artefact and owner. Most people live in homes that have collections of items representing a span of many years. In most people's minds there is a similar muddle of past, present and future. As a general rule as people age so they live more in the past, because they have so many more memories and their response to change slows or dulls. This is not universally true. Some older people are revolutionaries, some young fogies deliberately conservative. Some middle-aged people in senior roles are more in touch with the cutting edge of change than many younger people.

The man who is the most passionate opponent of class, hierarchy and inherited privilege may also be the staunchest defender of his rural views. He wants some types of change but not others. The woman who wants promotion at work, a change of job, may be fighting to keep her family together. She is against change at home.

The present generation in power, my generation, the 40-somethings are on the whole proud of their youth. They still seem to think 60s style is modern. They recreate the pop music, the car styles, the permissive climate of their teenage years. Their idea of modern is more archaic than anarchic, more sentimental than radical.

How history shapes a nation

So what then is the nation? Why is Britain a nation? Can Scotland and Wales be called nations again? Why is Europe not yet a nation? Can it ever be? The answer lies in the past. The past is not another country, but a defining part of present countries. Changing the past means adding the present. It means changing the perspective of a people about its past. It means adjusting the focus of a nation's glasses.

Just as individuals time-travel, so do nations. British people do not travel as part of a European nation, because we have not lived in one before. Memories of the Roman occupation are not a part of our daily experience, and we might not be that well disposed to the legions if we studied them more carefully. We have a more vibrant memory of the last few hundred years, and our strongest memory is of the last few decades. The US nation has little collective memory of events on the continent before the arrival of the Pilgrim Fathers.

Collective memories are like grains of sand. They build up on the beach of the nation. They can be buried and shifted, forgotten, or regarded from a different vantage point, but not destroyed. They are there for rediscovery. A nation has a mood, a feeling, that at times burns brightly. Are national memories as strong as family ones? Are they to be compared?

Each nation has its own symbols, ceremonies, traditions and colours. These emblems become important when there is conflict over what constitutes a nation. In 1939, Welsh and English, Scottish and Northern Irish agreed that Hitler and all he stood for was evil. They rallied to the red, white and blue of the Union flag. There was agreement that the UK had to stand for democracy and the self-determination of peoples against the force of German imperialism and racism. That conflict defined our nation's values sharply. Victory allowed us to write a chapter of European history, and ask that others saw the changes of 1945 when democracy triumphed as good in itself. We did not then create a united European nation, but took pride in how Britain had stood alone, and then with US help, for a common cause.

People can no more lay aside their past than a snail can shed its shell. Nor can a nation cast it off. A nation carries its past like a snail its house. Any nation which tries to shake off the shell is vulnerable to breakdown and attack. Revolutionary eras shake off the past only to provoke civil wars and reaction. Revolutionary change still cannot purge a country of all its history, it can only suppress and distort it. Revolutionary Russia changed all the place-names, rewrote the history books, tried to suppress the religion of the people and the culture of the Tsars, only to see its work reversed with the collapse of communism. Today, the greatest pride in Moscow is in the great buildings of the Kremlin, the home of the old ruling dynasty. At the heart of France is a hole where the monarchy and Church once stood. The Catholic Church has not been eliminated by the atheistic outlook of the Jacobins. The elected presidency has adopted some of the trappings of the old monarchy it replaced, and pursues through its monumentalism the search for a centralised secular governmental soul.

Britishness is similarly bound up with the past. In the 1940s and 1950s it was easy to define the British. Mother and father were married and stayed together. Large areas of the world were coloured red on the maps. Large-scale immigration into Britain from the New Commonwealth had not started. British people travelled proudly around the world after the war despite the poverty and drabness. People were born into a world of settled values. These were to be shattered or questioned by what happened next. The sexual revolution undermined the conventional family. The arrival of people from all over the world led to a multi-ethnic Britain.

The idea of Britishness transformed itself into the embracing identity of today. Many felt ill at ease as families were rent asunder from within, and the old nations of the UK started to bridle at the union from without.

The past is there in the landscape. The Roman occupation left straight roads like Fosse Way and Watling Street, villas and forts, grid-iron patterned towns, coins and artefacts. The French invasion of William the Conquerer in 1066 left us Battle Abbey, the White Tower of London and some of our government machinery. The attempted invasion by the Spaniards in 1588 is commemorated in the Armada train that departs daily from Plymouth, in the tourist attractions of that city and in our folklore and history. The Catholic powers' attempt to kill the king and change our religion in 1605 is remembered annually on Bonfire Night. Napoleon's failure to conquer us is there for all to see at Waterloo Station and in Trafalgar Square, celebrating the two most famous British victories of the long Napoleonic Wars. The defeat of the German invasion plans in 1940 is relived through many a war movie, there are war memorials to the dead in every town and village, and statues to the great military leaders in London.

The history of Britain in Europe

Britishness is bound up with this difficult relationship with Europe. The first millennium after the birth of Christ saw the country regularly pillaged, conquered and settled by marauders from elsewhere in Europe. Romans, Normans, Danes, Angles, Saxons – all made their mark. The second millennium saw a nation emerge, founded on liberty and a sense of justice, that fought off threats to its independence by making good use of the moat around these islands. Our defeats of France, Spain, Holland and Germany during the second millennium prevented any one power becoming dominant on the continent. After we gave up Calais we spent 500 years fighting European wars; not for conquest of territory, but to keep the balance of power. We usually allied with the smaller and weaker powers against the greater.

Those who want us to be fully engaged in Europe have usually had their way. We were regularly at war on the continent. We were again in the 1990s in the Balkans. In the twentieth century, British lives were lost in two world wars, in the Spanish and Russian civil wars and in lesser conflicts on the continent. We have twice had to remodel Europe with our US allies, through the Treaty of Versailles and at Potsdam after the Second World War.

Should Britain have been this committed? How would we have fared if we had not plunged into the First World War? What if we had intervened to stop Hitler earlier? Would there have been a Hitler at all if the UK and the US had not helped France to such a comprehensive victory in 1918? Could it be that some of our military intervention made it worse, not better?

The UK could have followed a maritime strategy of constructive disengagement from continental land battles. If we had fewer ambitions to influence the direction of events on the continent we could have defended these islands at less cost to ourselves in lives and treasure. Why do we want all this influence? Is it significant that the Liberal government which led us in the First World War through such atrocious losses was the last Liberal government? Perhaps the people never forgave them for the slaughter and the sense of futility captured in the songs and poems of that era.

The thesis that Britain had to stop hostile occupation of the Low Countries is flawed. There is limited truth in the idea that the

Channel ports are a pistol loaded and pointed against England's soft southern underbelly, the Thames estuary and the Kentish coast. The idea that we could stop hostile occupation of Calais and Dunkirk by continental military intervention is not well based in historical events. After the return of Calais to France in the mid-sixteenth century the nearest Channel ports have remained in French hands, and France has often been hostile to Britain. They never succeeded in using them to launch a successful invasion. For many years in the seventeenth century the Dutch challenged Britain's supremacy at sea. They did not succeed in mounting a successful opposed invasion, although the political leaders of Britain did invite in a Dutch king and queen as a solution to an internal British crisis in 1688. The transfer of Belgium from one owner to another until its establishment as a separate country did little to damage Britain.

For Britain has been defended by three physical, mental and military barriers. The first is the Channel which has proved such a formidable barrier to invaders. Channel tides and winds helped to destroy the Armada. Napoleon never dared put his barges to sea. Hitler gave up when he failed to control the air and sea.

The second line of defence has been the Royal Navy, and more recently its air arm. Many continental imperialists thought better of it when they saw the force of Britain at sea and more recently in the air. The Royal Navy was crucial in destroying the Armada with fireships. Napoleon knew his ships could not see off the Royal Navy. Hitler failed to win the battle for air supremacy, let alone naval supremacy to allow the invasion forces to cross.

The third line of defence is the spirit of the British people. 'Britons never, never, never shall be slaves' is written in the hearts of many. Britain would fight street by street were any continental power foolish enough to invade and strong enough to get across the narrow straits.

Had we kept out of the First World War we would probably have maintained our empire for longer. Had we relied on sea and air power we could have defended ourselves and left the French and Germans to fight over the future of the continent. We were weakened by the First World War. We were late to intervene as Hitler rose to power. The effort needed to crush him by the 1940s was enormous. It led to an early collapse of our influence in many other parts of the world after 1945, and to an easier assumption by the US of first-power status. We have paid dearly for our European entanglements. It is easier to argue we have been too involved in Europe, than to argue that we have not been involved enough.

US nationalism and understated British nationalism

The British Union has been much less bombastic about itself in the last 50 years than the US. It is never easy holding together very large countries, even where there is military and imperial success, a common language, and other obvious means of keeping people together. The idea of US nationalism is sold daily to the US people. Whenever you visit someone in authority in the US there is always the Stars and Stripes flag in his or her room. For all main public celebrations, red, white and blue is predominantly used in the balloons and the bunting, and even the drum majorettes would usually be dressed in patriotic colours. Every young American is taught the wonders of the Constitution, and encouraged to express loyalty to the aims of the founding fathers of the United States of America. The oath of allegiance has only just been dropped as a compulsory opener to the school day. New arrivals in the US are encouraged to learn English as the way to gain a job and get on in the world. Most of the volunteers that go to the US willingly sign up to the US idea of self-help through capitalism. Indeed, that is often the reason most go there in the first place.

There is no such constant repetition of the brand of Britain in British education or in British life. The British are curiously reticent now about expressions of Britishness. The adoption of the national flag as a symbol by an extreme party in British political life has made many people nervous of using their own flag for more emollient purposes. It is a great pity that people are put off using our flag, but understandable when they feel that some of the people brandishing it are connected with hooliganism or even racism.

The understatement of British life is clear in any ministerial office. No flags are ever stood in the corners of the rooms, and British government is remarkably undemonstrative about its belief in Britishness or its wish to promote it. History teaching in schools now seems keener to undermine the achievements of Empire and of the British by offering many timely reminders of the mistakes that were made, rather than seeking to show that British achievement around the world was notable. Devolution has taken hold in many of our schools. In Welsh schools there is a passionate wish to teach the Welsh language and to give children an independent sense of Welsh identity. In Scottish schools, Scottish history and Scottish attitudes predominate where once British views were more prevalent. The English are beginning to think of retaliation with growing signs now of English nationalism in teaching south of the border, but with that same English sense of understatement and self-criticism which characterises the race.

Team sports are very important ways of organising senses of identity. In the United States people are desperately keen to see US teams do well around the world, and to see US athletes scoop the pool when it comes to gold medals in the Olympics and other international sporting meetings. The British have never had the same sense of Britishness through sport, despite the fact that the British are a very sporting race who have exported a large number of interesting games to the rest of the world, only to see the rest of the world play them considerably better than many British teams are able to do.

It has been accepted in British life that most of the sporting activity takes place in the old nations that predated the Union. Intense rivalry between Ireland, Scotland, Wales and England is prevalent in soccer, in rugby and in many other team sports. One of the great national games is cricket. Welsh people willingly play as part of the English team. Scottish people have usually kept their distance from the whole idea, although in the most recent world cricket competition Scotland fielded a promising looking side of its own. In rugby, most passion is given to developing the individual home teams of Scotland, Wales, England and Ireland. It is the one aberration in Irish life where Northern Irish and southern Irish come together and play under the same Irish colours. The British Lions have their day and have their successes, but they do not attract the same degree of sustained passion as the individual national teams. In soccer, many fans are left wondering what a British team would look like and where it might rank in the world. For the last 30 years separate teams of England, Scotland, Wales and Ireland have not been that successful. No one could imagine the US fielding four or five different teams from different parts of that large country. Nor could anyone now imagine the Federal Republic of Germany fielding four or five teams representing the larger federal states within their union.

If we were serious about developing and treasuring British identity we would do rather more to develop British sporting teams and to field them internationally. The presence of a British soccer team, the more sustained presence of the British Lions in the world of rugby, and the development of a British cricket team could make quite a difference to popular perceptions of where true loyalties lay. The antipathy between the old nations within the Union can be so great that many a Scot would willingly cheer for an opposing foreign team against England, especially if Scotland has itself been eliminated from the international competition.

A sign that the Union is not all dead comes from the English who would nearly always cheer the Scottish, the Welsh or the Irish team in circumstances where England has been eliminated and where one of the other home teams was going on and meeting foreign competition to try to win the trophy. It is easier for people from the dominant part of the Union to feel relaxed about the Union, but it is also important for those who wish the Union to survive that this remains so.

A sense of European identity is slow to emerge. In English schools children feel overwhelmingly British. It nails the lie of federalists that we are to plunge into a European Union for the young people who feel themselves to be more European than British. The younger generation is more enthusiastically British and less European in its sensibilities than the parental generation that preceded them. This is not surprising, as young people do not regularly travel to the continent on business to trade in the way that the middle-aged generation does. Young people in the true British tradition wrestle with foreign languages with considerable difficulty. The language barrier is probably the main impediment to a greater sense of European identity and to more exchange and conversation across the Channel.

The advent of cheaper air travel has begun to change people's travel patterns as well. In the 1970s and 1980s the package holiday market opened up travel to Spain, to Italy and to France for a large number of people who had not travelled abroad before. More recently, the advent of good-value transatlantic fares has opened up the US to many more visitors. Many British people prefer to travel the long distance across the Atlantic than the short distance across the Channel because they feel more at home in an English-speaking culture.

Summer gives government Ministers the opportunity to travel abroad to promote British exports, to work with British companies and to learn how others do things. There is always a long queue of requests for Ministers to visit the US, Canada, Australia, New Zealand and English-speaking Asia. Few want to visit Bonn or Frankfurt or Paris or Rome. On one occasion the Foreign Office sent round a memo saying that it could not accept any more visitors to the US, but it urgently required people to go to the major European capitals to give some sense of our Europeanness and some encouragement to our partners.

The reluctance of senior, well educated people in governments wishing to be more European to travel to European destinations spoke volumes about how those people see themselves in practice. Although their head – the prime minister and the Foreign Office – tells them they should feel and be European, their heart and their instincts drag them across the Atlantic. In many ways the Atlantic is a narrower divide than the Channel.

Some making footfall for the first time in the US are amazed by its differences, but many see a familiarity of outlook and approach. The shared history is everywhere to be seen. In some ways the US has preserved eighteenth-century Britain rather better than Britain herself. Some roads are still called turnpikes. They still have a means of impeaching their elected monarch when we have lost the process of impeachment against the evil councillors of our government. They have preserved more of the vitality and independent spirit of the Protestant and Puritan religion than we have succeeded in doing in apathetic Britain. The very architecture of Washington is a perfect model of the European revival of classicism that came from the grand tours and the fevered study of Greco-Roman artefacts and fragments.

What, then, are we to make of ourselves as a mongrel people who have spread our influence so widely around the world, and now find the world coming back to spread its influence on us? As we eat our curry and rice, or contemplate going to buy sweet and sour pork at the local Chinese restaurant, are we British, European or English? As we read our English-language newspapers about the sex scandal in the presidency, watch old US movies and enjoy US comedies imported by our television companies, are we Little Americans, or are we still Europeans? As we sit in a street café, freezing out of doors (because that is how the Italians do it), drinking a cappuccino, planning a package holiday to Spain for the summer, but speaking in English and paying in sterling, are we British or are we Europeans? Are the cappuccino and street café culture just signs that mongrel Britain can absorb influences from everywhere? Why should the street café and the cappuccino be more influential in defining our identity than the McDonald's or the Coke float? If we go to Disneyland in Paris, are we going because we like the US cultural achievement, or because we like Paris, or because we like both, or because we are simply muddled? Do we have to be careful in case regressing to Scottish, English and Welsh identities makes it very difficult for many new Britons who have arrived over the last 40 years from various countries and climes? Could Englishness, or Welshness, be an inclusive identity, as successful as British in absorbing new peoples and creating a polyglot new culture?

The US has been a great melting pot by insisting on compulsory Americanisation. Whilst New York is still split into a dozen different districts, preserving much of the cultural origins of its people – the Italian area, the Spanish area, and so forth – the rest of the US is more united, showing the success of a policy based on one flag, one anthem, one central bank, one government, one language and one idea of nationhood. Britain has been more relaxed or more careless about its idea of nationhood. Into the cultural and educational vacuum that is sometimes being created, new nationalisms are being poured. The present British establishment does not believe in Britain and is actively encouraging, or conniving in, the destruction of Britishness by the forces of Europeanisation from without, and devolution from within. This is a time for Britain to start making some decisions. It is time for people to decide for themselves whether they value being British and if so, whether they are going to do something to define a new Britain for the new century.

All of us living in the present with hopes for the future are nonetheless the product of a whole series of influences and ideas from the past. It is to this heavy and rich legacy of our nation's past and to the great exponents of the rival futures that we must now turn in pursuit of an answer to which road Britain should follow.

2
A United States of Europe or a Union of English-Speaking Peoples: Two Rival Models for the US and Britain

Churchill's vision of Britain, Europe and the US

Winston Churchill set out his view of the development of a United Europe and the eventual union of the English-speaking peoples in two crucial speeches in 1946. The first was delivered on 5 March at Westminster College, Fulton, Missouri. In it he paid tribute to the enormous power of the US and the way that power was used to further democratic purposes around the world. He regularly associated the UK with US aims and constantly referred to the English-speaking peoples.

Churchill set out the task for the English-speaking peoples over the years ahead. He said that together we must stand up for 'the safety and welfare, the freedom and progress, of all the homes and families of all the men and women in all the lands'. He wanted the US and Britain to stand against tyranny, war and famine. He called upon the US to back his plan for United Nations forces to reinforce the new organisation to keep world order. He drew attention to the great common tradition between the US and Britain when he said:

> we must never cease to proclaim in fearless tones the great principles of freedom and the rights of man which are the joint

inheritance of the English-speaking world and which through Magna Carta, the Bill of Rights, the habeas corpus, trial by jury, and the English Common Law find their most famous expression in the American Declaration of Independence.

In a moving passage, he pledged:

all this means that the people of any country have the right, and should have the power by constitutional action, by free unfettered elections, with secret ballot, to choose or change the character or form of government under which they dwell; that freedom of speech and thought should reign; the course of justice, independent of the Executive, unbiased by any party, should administer laws which have received the broad assent of large majorities or are consecrated by time and custom. Here are the title deeds of freedom which should lie in every cottage home, here is the message of the British and American peoples to mankind.

Churchill's aim was common citizenship between the United Kingdom and the US. He called upon the US in this epoch-making speech of 1946 to grant a special relationship between the British Commonwealth and Empire and the United States. He said, 'for eternal association requires not only the growing friendship and mutual understanding between our two vast but kindred systems of society, but the continuance of the intimate relationship between our military advisers, leading to common study of potential dangers, similarity of weapons and manuals of instructions, and to the interchange of officers and cadets at technical college'. The US and UK should use each other's bases and provide mutual military security. He foresaw, 'eventually there may come the principle of common citizenship that we may be content to leave to destiny, whose outstretched arm many of us can already clearly see'.

In the rest of the speech Churchill revealed the threat as he saw it from communism. His memorable phrase about an iron curtain descending across the continent was so strong that it has taken people's minds away from the leading theme and main opening of the speech, urging the English-speaking peoples to a stronger union. Churchill looked forward to a world 50 years on where he would see:

seventy or eighty millions of Britons spread about the world and united in defence of our traditions, our way of life, and of the world causes which you and we espouse. If the population of the English-speaking Commonwealths be added to that of the United States with all that such co-operation implies in the air, on the sea, all over the globe and in science and in industry, and in moral force, there will be no quivering, precarious balance of power to offer its temptation to ambition or adventure. On the contrary, there will be an overwhelming assurance of security.

Churchill passionately believed that only the US and Britain standing strong side by side could see off the communist threat and persuade Russia not to open another war.

The parallel speech on the tragedy of Europe was delivered at Zurich University on 19 September 1946. Churchill drew a contrast between Christian faith, Christian ethics, culture, arts, philosophy and science that had come from Europe over the centuries with the 'series of frightful nationalistic quarrels originated by the Teutonic nations, which we have seen even in this twentieth century and in our own lifetime, wreck the peace and mar the prospects of all mankind'. He was stirred by the vision of famine, tyranny, migrating peoples, desolation and destruction. Churchill never wanted to see such desolation and despair again. His remedy was very simple. He wished to make all the continent of Europe or the greater part of it as free and happy as Switzerland. He decided the way to do this was 'to recreate the European family, or as much of it as we can, and provide it with a structure under which it can dwell in peace, safety and in freedom. We must build a kind of United States of Europe.'

Throughout the speech Churchill was careful to stress that the British were in a different position with their Commonwealth of Nations. He went on to say, 'The first step in the recreation of the European family must be a partnership between France and Germany. In this way only can France recover the moral leadership of Europe. There can be no revival of Europe without a spiritually great France and a spiritually great Germany.' A United States of Europe would reduce the strength of any individual European state, and give small nations an important part in its constitution. He sketched the idea of a federal United States of Europe based upon the four freedoms that President Roosevelt had set out. It would be achieved by forming a

Council of Europe led by France and Germany. The speech ends in a conclusive way, 'Great Britain, the British Commonwealth of Nations, mighty America, and I trust Soviet Russia – for then indeed all would be well – must be the friends and sponsors of the new Europe and must champion its right to live and shine.'

No one reading these speeches could be in any doubt about Churchill's aim. Churchill categorically wanted a United States of Europe involving only the continental powers. He was assured that Britain, with its Commonwealth and Empire, was one of the big players and would remain so. He was passionately committed to an ever greater rapprochement between Britain and the US, seeing the growing dominance of the US stretching ahead. He was well aware that the US had the keys to the nuclear bomb technology shared between Britain, the US and Canada. He was very keen that this technology should not fall into hostile communist hands and that the breathing space granted by the technical lead should be used to create a strong English-speaking union that could police freedom and democracy around the world. Churchill sowed the seeds of an idea which still has relevance today, as the US begins to question its enthusiasm for a United Europe including the UK.

Kohl, Chirac and EU views of the future

Despite the clarity of these comments, those seeking to build a United States of Europe have constantly quoted the one phrase from Churchill which, when taken out of context, could lead people to believe that he wanted Britain to be part of this new structure. There is no better place to start in seeing this misquotation than in the works of former Chancellor Helmut Kohl, far and away the most influential of the European political leaders of the 1980s and 1990s, keen to establish a federal United States of Europe. In 1991 Chancellor Kohl delivered an important address to Edinburgh University when receiving an honorary doctorate there. Kohl set out his vision of unity in diversity for Europe. He stated, 'for many reasons, not least geographical and historical ones, we as Germans are particularly keen to see Europe become more and more integrated.' He went on to quote Churchill's phrase about a kind of United States of Europe with approval. Kohl's speech is littered with assumptions that Britain will be part of this common structure. He nowhere refers to the obvious sense of Churchill's speech that Britain would not.

Where Kohl and Churchill did agree was in seeing a United States of Europe on the continent as being some kind of guarantee that there would be no more nationalistic wars. To Kohl, 'Germany unity and European union were two sides of the same coin.' The Edinburgh speech pointed in two directions at the same time. The audience was assured by the German Chancellor that Germany would not become eastward-looking but would remain firmly bedded in the West. On the other hand, the speech proudly pointed out: 'Krakow is the centre of Europe and Prague and Budapest are at the heart of Europe.' Chancellor Kohl was always determined that not only were the two Germanies to reunite quickly, but Poland, Hungary and Czechoslovakia should rapidly gain admission to the EU.

Kohl also believed the EU would be developed and furthered by the strengthened powers of the European Community itself. He stated in the Edinburgh speech, 'European stability largely depends on being able to enhance the scope for action of the Community both internally and externally.' He always sought not only economic and monetary union, which he won for the continental countries in the Treaty of Maastricht, but also political union, which emerged somewhat watered down from the Treaty of Amsterdam. Kohl sought a common foreign and security policy leading on to a common defence policy. He and his advisers felt that within a decade there would be a common European army able to enforce it. He stated at Edinburgh, 'we vitally need a common European police force that would be able to operate without let or hindrance in all the Community countries'. Chancellor Kohl sought much wider powers for the European Parliament, a European currency, a single European interest rate, more common regional policies, a European criminal justice policy, common frontiers and immigration controls, a single passport, a single foreign policy – in summary, he wanted a federal super-state, including the UK. His Edinburgh speech was less reassuring to his British audience than he had perhaps hoped, although it was on reflection wise that he delivered it in Scotland rather than in a more Eurosceptic part of the UK.

Kohl took his thinking further when he made an important speech on European union on 17 May 1992, when presenting the Konrad

Adenauer prizes. This was one of his boldest statements of his enlarged vision for a united Europe. He stated:

> in Maastricht we laid the cornerstone for the completion of a European Union. The process leading to this objective is irreversible. We have shown with our contribution that united Germany is actively assuming its responsibility in and for Europe.

European federalists led by Kohl were always keen to show that the thing was inevitable and irreversible. Kohl's thesis was that a united Germany greatly enlarged by the addition of the eastern *Länder* and representing a colossal part of the population and geography of central and Western Europe had to be bound in to this new European super-state. He felt that only by this process could German power and influence be harnessed for a greater good and the interests of the smaller countries around taken properly into account. His careful choice of the words 'irreversible' and 'responsibility' are part of this theme.

To Kohl, the Treaty on European Union marked the beginning of a new and decisive phase in the process of European unification, that in a few years would lead to the completion of that for which Konrad Adenauer, Jean Monnet and Robert Schuman – as well as other fathers of modern-day Europe – had laid the foundation. Kohl was always worried that momentum or progress towards an integrated Europe was going to falter. There are always countries out to get a better deal, and there was always the problem of Britain seeking to veto progress. Momentum had to be achieved and an impression of rapid progress was created through speeches and decisions. It was also important in Kohl's view to root it in some sense of an evolving past. The EU needed its heroes, its guides and its progenitors, and they had to be regularly lauded. Figurative candles were lit to their memory, rooms and buildings were named after them as the European Union created its own sense of history and subtly attempted to have the whole history of Europe rewritten as a progress towards its ultimate consummation in a European Union. Charlemagne, other Holy Roman Emperors, and even Napoleon, jostle with Monnet and Schuman in the temples of European togetherness.

Kohl asserted that at Maastricht we agreed a political as well as an economic and monetary union. This was the most contentious part of the whole Maastricht negotiations. Britain and some other countries had vigorously resisted the idea that on top of a single currency the member states had to sign up to the effective integration of everything else – the completion of the EU that Kohl had always sought. The ink was scarcely dry on the Maastricht Treaty with its much-watered-down general provisions for political union before Kohl and his advisers were briefing that the process was nonetheless irreversible and that Maastricht represented an important movement in that direction. For Germany and for Kohl, political union was the prize and monetary union merely the instrument and the sacrifice to France to bring it all about.

Foreign policy

In his Munich speech Kohl revealed exactly what political union entailed.

> First of all, formulation of a common foreign policy. In the course of the next few years the Union will be speaking with a single voice on all major foreign policy matters and in particular it will be undertaking joint foreign policy action.

The idea of a common foreign policy was bitterly fought by Britain and some others. Britain was naturally worried about its special arrangements with the US and wanted to keep British security firmly based on NATO and the US alliance. Nonetheless, the British government conceded the principle of a foreign policy spokesman and a common European line where it could be agreed by unanimity. Germany and France wished to press on, desperately seeking the common foreign policy achieved by qualified majority voting and enforced by strong personality.

European army

Kohl also believed that 'a European security and defence identity will need to be formed ... This initiative is not directed against anyone. On the contrary, our European partners are invited to take part in this project.' France and Germany were tiring of the slow progress being made by the other member states, especially Britain. As Kohl told his audience, they had gone ahead with a joint army corps, a clear indication that they wished to create a common European army, navy and air force. The rather crude comment that the initiative was not directed against anyone did little to reassure people. It was clearly not directed against Russia itself, towards whom Kohl always pursued a very friendly policy. Russia understood that it was the US and NATO rather than the common European army that it should worry about. If anything, the initiative was directed against the UK, reluctant to come alongside this very important major step towards the creation of a super-state in place of a common market.

Common criminal laws

After making some noises aimed at a reassurance that the US would still be important and the transatlantic relationship still mattered, Kohl expatiated on his third area, 'integrating the core areas of interior and justice policy'. He sought a European police force to fight drug abuse and organised crime. He was after a common asylum and immigration policy. In this crucial set of areas Kohl was well ahead of German opinion, as his speech made clear. Germans shared some of the British fears about having immigration and criminal justice matters settled internationally rather than nationally. Germany feared that it would mean even more people crossing its permeable frontiers and less strict control than the German nation might exert for itself. The idea of a European police force was broached to fight obvious transnational criminal problems, where Kohl thought he could get most support from other countries. The intention, however, clearly went much deeper, and was part of a process of trying to create a powerful European state backed by a strong police presence.

A stronger European Parliament

His fourth aim was 'to improve the ability of the European Parliament to impose democratic controls on the European Commission authorities in Brussels ... In Maastricht we undertook important steps in this direction, however, this was not enough.' Kohl allowed himself another sideswipe at the inadequacies of the Maastricht Treaty where he had failed to convince all his partners of the need for rapid and urgent progress. Britain and France were both reluctant to see a strengthened European Parliament, preferring the power to reside around the Council of Ministers' table in the hands of elected ministerial politicians answerable to some extent to their national parliaments rather than the European one.

After urging immediate discussions to broaden EC membership from the twelve to include Austria, Sweden and Finland, Kohl said that at the same time institutional strengthening had to take place in the EC. In this, Kohl spoke on the correct side of the European debate about whether a widening of the Community, and expansion in its number of members, would lead to a loosening or a strengthening of central control. Kohl was quite clear that it had to lead to a strengthening of central control as it had done at the time of previous enlargements. Events proved Kohl to be right, and those British Eurosceptics who thought that a widening would lead to a loosening were once again thwarted. Kohl had to deal with the growing German disillusion with the idea of the abolition of the Deutschmark. He told the European peoples that a common European currency 'will open up numerous freedoms and, as such, expand horizons'. He wanted the common currency to be just as stable as the Deutschmark. He claimed credit for having put into the Maastricht Treaty a central bank modelled on the Bundesbank. This, he told his audience, would guarantee that stability.

We now know that events turned out rather differently. Over the first year of its life the European Central Bank, whilst using German structures, adopted a rather loose monetary policy which has led to a rapid devaluation of the external value of the Euro. The European Bank may well have as little political influence over it as the German one and have a certain kind of independence put into its statutes. Unfortunately, it has not presided over a stable currency in the way that the Bundesbank did for many years. The conclusion to Kohl's speech summed up his general message over his lifetime at the head of European politics.

The European unification process has been a key factor in the history of the Federal Republic of Germany. Only if we continue to pursue this course consistently will we continue to be successful in Germany, in a strong and united Europe. We remember what Konrad Adenauer said in his memoirs: 'in my view the European nation states had a past, but no future. This applied in the political, the economic, and the social sectors. No individual European country was able to guarantee its people a secure future on its own strength.'

Kohl reminded his audience of a provision in the German basic law of 1949, the eventual unification of Europe in line with Churchill's vision.

German thinking externalised the problems they had had in constructing a democratic, free and peace-loving state onto the rest of Europe. One of the most contentious parts of Kohl's thought was his statement that we needed a European Union to prevent future wars. This reflected Churchill's thinking from a very different era. Whilst it was just about understandable that Winston Churchill, in the immediate aftermath of the war, was worried not only about the communist threat but also about the remote possibility of the resurgence of German nationalism, it is more difficult to understand why democratic leaders of free Germany in the 1980s and 1990s had the same kind of fear. Kohl's critics offered two different lines of attack on his thinking. One group, myself included, pointed out that democratic peace-loving Germany of the 1980s and 1990s was not likely to go to war or to seek aggressive control over other people's territory again. He was fighting a spectre. Other critics said that there were much better guarantees against such German action in the future through NATO, US involvement in Europe, and the United Nations Charter. Most of us felt that there was never any likelihood of Germany declaring war on its neighbours in the second half of the twentieth century. This was not because Germany had joined the Common Market or the EU, but because the whole structure of German and European politics had shifted decisively against such action.

Nonetheless, German thinking became dominant in the new Europe of the post-war world. The irony is that a structure invented by Churchill to deal with the futures of the devastated and defeated powers on the continent was transformed into an instrument for European Union, and subsequently came back to haunt the United Kingdom which had been carefully kept apart from any such proposal by Churchill. Many federally inclined British thinkers often quoted Churchill without bothering to read his speeches or realising that he wanted something very different from a United States of Europe where Britain was just one province among many. Churchill, I am sure, is turning in his grave as a result of what has now happened with the reunification of Germany, the sidelining of the Commonwealth and the failure to follow through the move to union which he started in his special relationship with the US.

Kohl's legacy lives on and now shines even brighter. The present German Foreign Minister, Herr Fischer, is a strong proponent of 'political union', the remodelling of Europe as a single federal state along German lines. President Chirac of France wishes a core of European countries to rush forward to something more like a centralised French state. Kohl's candle has become a brazier, inflaming the European skies.

The attitude of France

On 27 June 2000, Jacques Chirac, president of France, made an important speech to the German Bundestag. Chirac said that the division of Germany was a tragic parenthesis in the story of unification of Germany and the continent. He began in high-flown phrases, praising German unity and the return of the capital to Berlin. As the first foreign head of state to address the whole of Germany, he expressed delight at the huge change in France's former adversary. He chronicled how Konrad Adenauer and General de Gaulle worked together to create a Franco-German alliance, how this was strengthened by Willi Brandt and Georges Pompidou, continued by Helmut Schmidt and Valéry Giscard d'Estaing, and developed further by Helmut Kohl with François Mitterrand. Chirac sees the European Union as 'the world's leading economic and trading power'. He sees it as 'a research and innovation giant', greatly strengthened by the adoption of the Euro as part of the unification process. He points out that the EU is making its voice heard well beyond its borders, and he welcomes the development of a separate EU foreign and security policy. Chirac looks forward to the arrival of Europe as 'a world power in which majority voting is the rule and which reflects the relative weights of the member states'. He is keen on developing an inner or pioneer group of states clustered around Germany and France that will take the process of political integration forward much more quickly. The immediate task he wishes to undertake is a central economic policy, a stronger defence and security policy and a common fight against crime amongst the pioneer group. Chirac wants a European constitution setting out the functions of the different levels of government, and is an enthusiast for the charter of fundamental rights. Chirac praises new alliances in aerospace, chemicals, energy, insurance and services, and looks forward to more mergers and common working between French and German business.

Whilst some saw in the speech a little cooling of ardour compared with Herr Fischer's dramatic statement of the need for a United States of Europe, there is little in Chirac's words to comfort British politicians. Whilst Chirac may be more careful in how he explains his ambitions, looking behind him to the French audience as well as to the front to the German one he was addressing, the end result is the same. Chirac's idea of the united Europe is one which harnesses industrial, commercial and military power, has a single economic policy, a single currency, a single foreign policy and a combined military machine to back up that foreign policy stance.

Britain at the edge of Europe but at the centre of the world

In his Fulton, Missouri, speech, and in his writings generally, Churchill always stated that Britain, with its Empire – or Commonwealth, as imperial countries gained independence – should stand alongside the US and the newly united Europe as one of the big three influences upon future world development. Churchill was even more of a visionary. He looked forward to a day when British power, even with its Commonwealth and Empire, might not be sufficient on its own to fulfil these onerous responsibilities. He was quite clear in all his writings that the solution was a union of the English-speaking peoples.

Churchill's aims for the post-war world

Churchill the historian wrote *A History of the English Speaking Peoples*. He did not write 'A History of the European Peoples', which would have been the natural thing to do had he wished Britain to be part of a united Europe. The *History of the English Speaking Peoples* shows his love and enthusiasm for Australia, New Zealand, South Africa, the Indian sub-continent, the United States and Canada, as well as the home islands. Churchill felt that the ties of kinship, language and common governmental systems were such that it would be possible to bring these countries together in one large English-speaking union.

Nowhere in his speeches and writings does Churchill look forward to the modern world where mighty Asia emerges as the dominant force on the world landscape by dint of huge population and growing economic strength. Nowhere did Churchill forecast the enormous increase in the commercial power of Japan, nor did he contemplate what would happen when over a billion Chinese began to make some sensible decisions about their economic and political development and wished to have some influence in the world. It is possible that he dimly grasped what might happen to the relative size of Britain and even the US as these events unfolded. It may just have been that he had a powerful emotional tie to all of the territories of the former Empire and then the Commonwealth, such that he hoped one day on different terms the original Empire could be put back together again as an English-speaking union. This is the more likely explanation, given the passion of his campaigns to try to keep India in the Empire and his obvious reluctance to see its dismemberment.

So how realistic, then, would Churchill's aim be? In his writings he makes it clear that it should begin by a defence alliance or merger. Indeed, something along these lines has in practice occurred in the post-war world. Britain has become dependent on the US for the supply of weapons systems, technology and armaments, and there is a great deal of common procurement between the mighty US military machine and the rather smaller, but still very efficient, British one. British and US men in arms have regularly undertaken ventures together. Experiences shared and learned in the Second World War have continued through a series of engagements in the Middle East, in Asia, and now on the continent of Europe.

Churchill felt that things would then branch out from a defence and foreign policy alliance to a more wholehearted union. He thought it impossible from his vantage point in the middle of the twentieth century to forecast exactly how that would occur, but he seemed confident that the natural pressure of events would lead to some common destiny for the English-speaking peoples.

The case of European enthusiasts

European enthusiasts are equally confident that Britain's natural destiny is to be a full part of the United States of Europe now emerging from the various European treaties. The EU has come a long way from the early days of the Treaty of Rome and the Messina Conference. Those who favour greater European integration always regret Britain's reluctance to grasp the agenda in the 1950s. Although Britain attended the Messina Conference to set up the EEC, the ministerial and Foreign Office line at the time was that a United States of Europe would never work and that Britain should not be part of it. Thus began Britain's agonies as it anguished over whether it should join, how it should join, and how far it should go in accepting the considerable degree of unification implied by successive treaties drafted at the behest of Germany and France.

Whilst it is still endlessly debated whether it would have been different or better had Britain gone to the Messina Conference with proposals of its own to shape the new Europe, there is little point now in crying over spilt milk. It is possible that had Britain offered leadership at the Messina Conference for a free-trade open Europe with less political integration and less law from Brussels, it might have had some influence. If, in the 1950s, 1960s and 1970s, Britain had stated consistently that Europe needed to be more open to the outside world and less regulated, it may have moved the position somewhat. The fact is that Britain made a decision in 1955 not to join and then subsequently regretted it. The 1960s were dogged by Britain's failure to persuade France that it should be allowed to join the newly strengthened EEC. When membership finally came in 1973, a large number of decisions had been made, treaties written, and a series of important diplomatic relationships established in the community of six which were difficult to break into. Since 1973, Britain has learnt in a painful way that the Community really is based upon a Franco-German alliance. As the years have rolled by, so the close-working cooperation between French and German government officials at all levels has been matched by the willingness of French and German leaders to meet before every EC then EU conference to sort out between them how they thought the debate and decisions should go. Britain has never succeeded in prising France and Germany apart on the big issues and has therefore been left with surprisingly little influence over the outcome of the Union's development.

Committed Euro-federalists say that a United States of Europe is not only inevitable but desirable. They see that the Parliament, Commission, Court, Bank, Court of Auditors, flag, anthem, common frontiers and all the rest are the building blocks of a new federal state. They believe that Britain's rightful and only place in the world is to be one of the important groups of regions within the new Europe of the regions. They think Britain might have a bit more influence over what comes next if it were more wholeheartedly committed, but the honest ones accept that the crucial decisions have now been taken and Britain has to make a decision whether to take it or leave it. Indeed, many committed Euro-federalists believe the choice is as stark as that. They do not believe it realistic for Britain to carry on doing what it has done over the last 25 years, reluctantly accepting some parts of the Union and refusing to join in on others. They believe that it will soon be impossible to dine à la carte in the Community and that a country will have to choose either to have the whole table d'hôte menu or to leave the dining room altogether.

The isolation of the UK in the EU

One of the things that strikes any travelling British person interested in these arguments when talking to the political and business elites on the Continent is how little understanding and sympathy for Britain's position there is. Indeed, Euroscepticism of any kind is often greeted with broad incomprehension, immediately followed by anger and petulance. The governing and corporate elites of Europe do not think Euroscepticism is a respectable political view. If a British voice expresses enthusiasm for European cooperation but insists on less law, less taxation, less regulation and less interference from Brussels, there is then a reluctance to sympathise followed by a powerful counter-argument. Anyone in Britain sceptical about the pace and size of government they are trying to create is made to feel unwelcome in many of the debates and seminars on the continent, as the juggernaut of European integration careers on its way.

It has been very difficult, if not impossible, for Britain to avoid being isolated. Over so many things Britain is naturally boxed into a corner. The origins of the dispute lie in a fundamentally different approach to nationhood and sovereignty. All British governments, whether right, left or centre, do believe that most important decisions about British life should be taken by the British government and debated in the British Parliament. All British governments find it difficult to square this with a strong and deeply felt wish on the part of continental politicians for more and more decisions to be taken by a bureaucracy in Brussels and not put through their own domestic parliaments.

The EU began as the *Club des Battus*. The defeated nations of Western Europe – including France, which had been defeated and put under German occupation for several years – decided there had to be a better way. Britain, a nation which had not been conquered or overrun for many centuries, did not share the fears and feelings of France and Germany, Italy and Belgium, Luxembourg and Denmark as they emerged from the Second World War. British politicians misread the strength of feeling and the likely developments on the Continent. They and their advisers felt that the EU would make very little progress. They felt that Britain could stand aloof, with its Empire, its Commonwealth and its strong US links. They dithered as to whether they welcomed the developments or not, and they dithered as to whether we should plunge in and shape them or not.

This ambivalence towards Europe is reflected in a whole series of political decisions and reverses over the last 50 years. It is reflected in the attitudes and outlook of many British people themselves. Many of us know that we are European, in the sense that Europe is our continent and that we live cheek by jowl with our French, Belgian and Scandinavian neighbours. Many of us know well that much effort and activity in our history has been taken up with the question of Europe, trying to settle relations with our at times ambitious, aggressive and warlike neighbours. There is in the British heart a wish that Europe should live at peace. Some also believe that a united Europe might be more likely to live in peace than a disunited one.

However, we are also an island people. We take pride in our centuries-long success as an independent country. We see that all previous attempts at European Union have been doomed. We know that most previous efforts to reunite Europe were based on military aggression and repression. Whilst we can see that this latest European project is proceeding by different means and in a different style, we have apprehensions that those who are driving it are going too far, too fast. There is a great danger that they are running ahead of popular opinion on the continent.

The importance of history to a nation's destiny

If you embark on a journey it is possible to conduct it in the present and future only. At any moment you can find your position by compass and observation. You can keep yourself pointing to your future destination. But that is not the only way, and not the way we usually choose to travel. We rely heavily on our sense of the past. We know where we started from, and where we have travelled through. When we pick up a map, we do not usually reach for the compass and the coordinates, we trace where we have been and know from that our direction of travel. As we pass through villages or past well known landmarks, we make a mental note of that past event to guide us on our future way. So it is with a nation and its collective consciousness. Britain has a particular kind of parliamentary democracy. In practice we can only understand why we have this particular version if we know how it has come to be created through past events. If we want to reform or improve, it is wiser to do so from an understanding of how it came about rather than from the imposition of a new set of principles.

Teaching is largely about passing on a corpus of knowledge from the past. It would take too long, and defeat too many, to expect a child to discover the universe anew for him- or herself. We are, as they said in the seventeenth century, dwarves standing on the shoulders of the giants so that we can see further. Teachers receive the wisdom of the past and pass it on to the present.

Much of our teaching is nationalistic, in the sense that it comes from a national rather than international tradition of knowledge. Understandably, in Britain children are taught in English, and English literature is the main recommended reading. Where teaching goes beyond the national tradition, it usually does so within an English-speaking framework. US works are more easily accessible to the British teacher than Russian or Chinese, or even French and German, ones.

Until recently, history has been written and viewed primarily from a national perspective. Most history teachers in British schools will not have read a history book written in any language other than English. Their only understanding of the different ways in which French, German, Italian or Spanish historians view European history will be based on the reading of foreign works by the authors of the English accounts they read. Practically no books of French, German or Spanish history have been translated into English for common use.

The difference in interpretation can be significant. To English students, Dunkirk is a British success. An army was rescued to defend Britain, and lived to fight another day. Victory in our story was plucked from the jaws of defeat. To the French, it was the British abandoning an ally and leaving France to the fate of certain Nazi occupation. It reflected British perfidy and incompetence, abandoning the French to themselves and the continent to the Germans. To the US it was a worrying event, but not one of such significance as the electrifying raid on Pearl Harbor.

To British students, Churchill's decision to scuttle the French fleet in Marseilles – to prevent the Nazis using it – once it was obvious the

French had lost was a resolute and important act. It showed that Britain had determination to resist the Germans and a strong sense of purpose. It would have been crazy to British minds to allow the Nazis to assemble an extremely powerful fleet and deploy it against Britain. To many Frenchmen it was the ultimate act of treachery, destroying the flower of the French navy after abandoning the French army in the north to the advance of the Nazis.

We see the same English-speaking-centred approach to more modern events. BBC news and current affairs programmes are dominated by events in Britain and the English-speaking world. The BBC will offer quite good coverage of a US presidential election campaign, but practically no coverage of a German or French election, which arguably now has a bigger impact on Britain than the US one given the number of decisions taken for us in Brussels by a Franco-German led administration. The BBC regularly runs news items of purely US national interest, plunging into US debates about property, race and abortion.

The BBC has been fascinated by apartheid and its abolition in South Africa and regularly presents programmes and features on South African society and politics. It has been mesmerised by the Truth and Reconciliation Commission, and has gone deeply into issues of South African economic progress or failure. I have never seen or heard a programme on the race problem in France, or the problems of poverty in Germany. The language barriers get in the way and the producers seem to lack interest. The whole way of thinking of successive generations of BBC producers is based on the English-speaking world, although the intention is usually to expose the weaknesses and failures in the English-speaking world whilst turning a blind eye or a deaf ear to any similar or worse weaknesses in the French- or German-speaking worlds. It is a kind of inverted bias, fascinated by the English-speaking world but determined to run it down wherever possible.

The new school of history is attempting to introduce a similar Eurocentric bias into their work, but it will take time for them to recruit a big enough army of historians to rewrite the whole history of these islands from a European perspective. Such a perspective would often regard Britain as either an irrelevance or an annoying nuisance on the periphery of the continent. Certainly, ever since the Henrician break from the Church of Rome in the 1530s there have been very different currents of development in the UK from those amongst the Catholic powers that have predominated on the continent. Where continental historians would see the sixteenth-century revolt of the Netherlands as an unfortunate episode, pulling apart political and religious union on the continent, English historians see it as a rather bold and successful attempt to free part of the Low Countries from the grip of Spanish and Habsburg control. Where many on the continent see Charlemagne and subsequent Holy Roman Emperors and Empire as a forerunner of the European Union, Britain sees the rupturing of the Holy Roman Empire as an improvement, creating more balance and diversity on the continent. We need to remember that countries like Germany and Italy that now sit around the ministerial table as unified were fractured into warring states and cities throughout most of the last millennium.

The endless wars, twisting alliances and changes of fortune in the 500 years that preceded our membership of the EU have been mirrored almost entirely in diplomatic and peaceful ways since we joined. The EU still maintains many of the old divisions of Europe around the ministerial table. Very often the Protestant countries find themselves in disagreement with the Catholic ones. A permanent disagreement between the southern Mediterranean countries and the northern countries is there for all to see. The smaller countries are often in disagreement with the larger countries and on a fairly regular basis, whether its prime minister is Harold Wilson, Jim Callaghan, Margaret Thatcher, John Major or Tony Blair, Britain ends up isolated and in disagreement with the lot. It will take a great deal of rewriting history, of changing the attitudes of British people towards freedom, democracy and self-determination, before this situation changes markedly.

Britain has drifted into its current position, perched precariously mid-Atlantic, subject to US commercial influences, on the one hand, and European political influences, on the other. It need not have been so. After winning the Second World War Britain was in a strong position to help fashion new alliances and a new architecture for Europe. Churchill set out his vision quite clearly in a series of important speeches. In Zurich, he thought the best solution was for France and Germany to merge. He wished them to join with the smaller countries and the defeated and crushed Western Europe to form a United States of Europe. He felt this was best for Franco-

German security and likely to prevent future wars. He also made it very clear that he did not think the UK need or should join such a grouping. Churchill always saw Britain as one of the big powers of the world – after all, Britain had apparently been an equal partner with the US and the Soviet Union in waging the war in Europe and then in settling the peace. Although Britain had had to commit a far larger proportion of its people and resources to the war effort than the US did to the war in Europe, and although Britain had been stretched by the global operations necessary for an imperial power, it had nonetheless more than pulled its weight and had an important influence over the decisions of the Peace Treaty and beyond. We must now turn to look at how the military relationship between the victorious Anglo-Saxon allies in 1945 has developed.

3
The US, the UK and the UN: The Special Relationship Policing the World

After the Second World War, the victorious powers decided there had to be a new attempt to impose some world order on the warring nations around the globe. In the immediate aftermath of the First World War in 1918 there were high hopes that the League of Nations would provide the answer. The League soon broke down, unable to tackle the aggressive intents of the new fascist and communist tyrannies which emerged in that fateful generation. There was less enthusiasm and more realism amongst the victor powers in 1945. Nonetheless, the Charter of the United Nations set out with high resolve to establish a framework of international law. It aimed at a new world order based upon the principles that had formed the substance of the Atlantic Declaration uniting Britain and the US at the height of the struggle. The Atlantic Declaration was the best statement of war aims produced during the conflict.

The foundation of the UN

The Charter of the United Nations decided it needed to 'save succeeding generations from the scourge of war'. It reaffirmed 'faith in fundamental human rights, in the dignity and worth of the human person, in the equal rights of men and women and of nations large and small'. It set out to promote social progress and better standards of life and to ensure that nations respected obligations arising under treaties. It urged nations to live tolerantly in peace with one another, to employ international machinery for the promotion of the economic and social advancement of all peoples, and to accept the idea that armed force should only be used in the common interest.

The UN intended to be a kind of international police force. It decided that the organisation would be based on the principle of the sovereign equality of all its members. All members have to agree to refrain from using force or the threat of force against the territory of any other state. The UN is above all based upon the principle of the self-determination of nations and peoples, one of the leading principles for which the Allies fought the Second World War.

The founding principles were heavily influenced by US rather than by British ideals. Indeed, some US thinkers and politicians were rather embarrassed that Britain still had such a large Empire in the 1940s. That is why, amongst other reasons, the Charter is laced with a strong stress on the individual rights and liberties of people in each state and upon the right of any nation to a separate existence. The Charter of the United Nations prevents its members from intervening in what are domestic matters within a nation but allows the organisation to intervene to save a small nation under pressure from an international aggressor, even where that aggressor believes that the small nation should rightly be absorbed into the larger whole.

The UN wrestled with the problem that it wished every country to be sovereign, to still have its own equal rights, but it also wished the new security architecture to be based upon the power reality of the modern world as it appeared after 1945. It hit upon the solution of every sovereign nation that so wished, to belong to the UN and meet in General Assembly, but with a special Security Council to deal with day-to-day matters and to make recommendations. The General Assembly of all the member nations can, under Article 10, 'discuss any questions or any matters within the scope of the present Charter ... and may make recommendations to the members of the United Nations or to the Security Council or to both on any such questions or matters'. The General Assembly is charged with the duty or the power to consider cooperation and the maintenance of international peace. The General Assembly receives annual special reports from the

Security Council, including accounts of the measures the Security Council has decided upon or taken to maintain international peace and security. The General Assembly approves the budget of the organisation, whilst the expenses are defrayed under a system of apportionment by all the members. Each national member of the General Assembly has one vote. Important decisions are made by a two-thirds majority, including recommendations with respect to the maintenance of international peace and security, the election of non-permanent members of the Security Council, election of members of the Economic and Social Council, the election of members to the Trusteeship Council, the admission of new members, the suspension of members, the expulsion of members and budgetary matters.

The UN Security Council

The Security Council is the main guiding hand of the UN. It consists of fifteen members. Five members are permanent members of the Council. China, France, USSR (now Russia) the UK and the US comprise the five permanent members. Each one of them has a veto over any matter coming before the Security Council. An additional ten members are elected by the General Assembly to represent the other nations. The idea was that the five most important military powers of the day would provide much of the military back-up to Security Council policy and therefore should have individually the right of veto over it. They can, however, be collectively out-voted by the ten other members who are elected from amongst the general body of the UN. The Security Council is required under the Articles to try to find a peaceful or negotiated answer to any problem before proceeding to the use of force. The Security Council can impose sanctions against countries breaking international law. Members of the UN are required through a separate agreement to make available agreed types of force should troops be needed. Before any member not represented on the Security Council has to provide armed forces for any Security Council proposal, that member may participate in the decisions of the Security Council concerning such deployment. In practice, countries remain in charge of whether or not their forces will be committed. Typical UN action is rather like summoning the Christian powers to a crusade. A general invitation is issued and volunteers are usually plentifully available.

The UN Economic and Social Council

In addition to its well known role as a world policeman, the UN was set up to promote higher standards of living, full employment, improved social, health, cultural and educational facilities, and universal respect for human rights. The Economic and Social Council consists of 54 members of the UN elected from the General Assembly. A number of ways of working are set out in general terms in the Articles. In practice, the UN has worked with a large number of governmental and non-governmental organisations in countries in need of assistance to improve health care and to promote economic progress and social justice.

Those countries who are signatories to the Treaty who retained colonies or dependent territories were guided under Articles 73 and 74 to develop self-government, to protect their subject peoples against abuse and to promote good neighbourliness. The UN also set up a trusteeship system to deal with states that had been held under mandate or had been detached from enemy states so-called, the countries which had lost the Second World War. The whole UN structure is backed up by the International Court of Justice (ICJ). Every member of the UN agrees to comply with any decisions of the ICJ and also provides its membership. The Court itself depends on 15 judges who have to be independent and come from different countries. They are elected by the General Assembly of the UN. The judges have to remain independent and the Court was established at The Hague.

The UN in practice

This complicated structure was designed with the immediate post-war circumstances very much in mind. Germany and Japan were still called the enemy countries. They were not to be part of the structure in the first instance. The victor powers decided that they could work together to deal with unforeseen but possibly dangerous problems likely to arise around the world as the incredibly complicated task of fitting the world back together was undertaken after years of war, bloodshed, devastation, mass migration and death. Hunger, poverty, ignorance, squalor and disease stalked the world. Humankind, through its own barbarism, had brought itself to a low point through unleashing so much high explosive. What is surprising about the UN, launched as the creature of its times against an unprepossessing background, is that it has lasted so long and in some ways has done so well.

Throughout much of the second half of the twentieth century there were those who thought the UN impotent to deal with the most pressing problem of the day, the danger of the Cold War between the Soviet Union and the United States breaking out into hot war through the clash of a democratic free system in the West and the communist system in the East. There is some truth in the argument that the containment of the Cold War owed much more to the attitudes of the US and the USSR than it did to anything the UN could do. The UN by definition is best at tackling smaller or medium-sized conflicts when the five large powers of the world, as defined by the Security Council, are in broad agreement about what should be done. There were numerous occasions in the Cold War period when this role was interrupted as the communist states and the democratic ones found themselves on opposite sides of the divide in the scramble for influence and authority around the world between these two competing systems. With the collapse of communism in 1990, many felt the UN would then come of age. In a way they were right, and in a way they were wrong. There are now more occasions when there is commonality of agreement around the Security Council table, but there are now also occasions when the overriding power of US weaponry is sufficient for the US effectively to sideline the UN and lead a moral and military crusade of its own.

People in the US are rather ambivalent about the whole idea of the UN. Some see it as the necessary guarantor of a world order providing a framework of international law. They accept the constraint it places upon a free foreign policy for the world's only superpower and are in sympathy with the objectives set out almost sixty years ago by the victorious powers. Others in the US resent the infringement upon the sovereign liberties of the US. They believe there is a necessary coincidence of US action and a moral cause, and can become impatient with the need on occasions to persuade the Security Council and the General Assembly that the US and its friends should intervene in the interests of peace or a more just settlement.

To British eyes the amount of sovereignty surrendered by the US or Britain in the UN is modest compared with the sacrifice of sovereignty the UK has made in joining the EU. Whilst theoretically under the United Nations Charter a country can be required to field its forces where it is not fully persuaded of the cause, in practice this does not arise. It can never even arise theoretically for the UK or the US as both have a veto on any Security Council proposals. In practice, armies, navies and air forces being committed to Security Council adventures are committed willingly by the member states. Any member state of the UN can resign its membership at the drop of a hat. For this, if for no other reason, no member state has to commit forces against its will.

In contrast, membership of the EU implies going along with the majority view in many areas and facing court sanctions if a country refuses to do so. It is not practical politics to withdraw from the EU just because one decision is not to a country's liking. Nor can a country negotiate non-compliance with a proposal just because it doesn't suit it. This is very different from the position of the UN where in practice all the important decisions are voluntary ones for an individual member state and are definitely voluntary ones for any of the big five. It is true that UN policy-making in other areas is at times vexatious from the Anglo-Saxon viewpoint. There is a need to restrain some UN agencies from becoming a proxy government for different parts of the world, and from over-zealous regulation.

It is possible to be optimistic about war and peace after 1945. Viewed from the perspective of the victorious powers Britain, the US, Russia and, in the later stages of the war, France, things have been a lot easier since then. None of these four powers has faced invasion or serious threat to its home territory since 1945. This contrasts with France being overrun by German invaders in 1940, Britain facing a full-blown air and sea-borne invasion threat, and Russia having to fight off one of the biggest and deadliest threats to its territory from the German army. In another sense the world has remained very strife torn. All too many disagreements and conflicts in the regions of the world have flared up into intense and often very damaging wars. British and US forces have been called upon to fight in Korea. The US made a huge military commitment to Vietnam. Britain had to fight to recapture the Falkland Islands; the US and British allies stood shoulder to shoulder to reclaim Kuwaiti independence from Iraq; a number of UN member countries and their forces have been committed to an endless series of disputes and wars in the Balkans, stretching from Croatia and Bosnia to Kosovo. The aim of the UN to sit everybody down and negotiate a settlement, has not proved possible in any of these cases. Nor has it been possible to bring countries and races to heel by applying sanctions. In each case UN member states have ended up as combatants trying to enforce a precarious peace on reluctant countries.

The world community has discovered that the simple distinction made in the United Nations Charter between military aggression against a sovereign state, on the one hand, and intervention in the home affairs of a sovereign state, on the other, has not been nearly as easy to make as they hoped. There are many more countries now than there were in 1945. One of the characteristics of the latter twentieth century was the splintering of former large countries as individual ethnic groups and sub-nations emerged, demanding their own autonomy and independence. This was something that the United Nations Charter was not really designed to tackle. The UN was born in a generation which saw the most likely threat as being the resurgence of military intentions by an aggressive major country wishing to invade its neighbours who were themselves clearly defined sovereign states. It is understandable that the French should have taken this view in the negotiations, as their sovereign nation had been several times invaded by their neighbours Germany. Instead, the most intractable problems in the world have been created by the ideological clash between communism and democracy, and more recently by racial tension. Each of these has posed problems that sometimes reach beyond the power of the UN to solve.

The muddle became very clear in the way the Western Allies approached the problems in Croatia, Bosnia and Kosovo. When the UN began its activities, the theory was that there would be humanitarian intervention only. Soldiers were sent out with white vehicles carrying the red cross insignia to convoy food and other necessary supplies to the affected populations, seeking free passage between the warring armies and guerrilla bands. As the conflict escalated, UN troops sometimes switched into full combat fatigues to maintain peace between the warring sides. On occasions they were attempting to keep a peace that had never been brokered. The soldiers were placed in a difficult position, often under orders to maintain a peace which the politicians, diplomats and negotiators had failed to establish. Occasionally, in desperation, the UN troops, often amounting to little more than NATO forces, were required to try to impose a military solution between two or more warring groups.

It has been discovered in these difficult situations that there can be no peace until the different peoples are prepared to live in the same community, or until the warring bands reach some kind of agreement or accommodation about some new set of frontiers and separate territories. We saw the pitiful sight of thousands of refugees on the roads of Eastern and central Europe as Serbian aggression was met by Muslim resistance. The UN has often had to look on powerless, relying primarily on the forces of NATO which in turn have rested predominantly on the forces of the US.

Pax Americana

Over the last 50 years we have seen the *Pax Americana*. In the tense years of the Cold War it was US diplomacy backed up by US technological superiority that created the balance of power with the communist world. Hot wars in Korea and Vietnam caused endless difficulties. US policy specialists debated the notion that they had to confront and roll back the communist advance through Asia. Some in the US believed in the domino theory – that the communists were going to move from island to island; from country to country; crossing borders; infiltrating the countryside; training guerrilla bands; providing support, ammunition and weapons from Russia and from China. They believed that only by confronting these forces in the field, offering full battle and putting a stop to the seemingly endless march of the communist troops, would the rest of the world be safe for democracy and freedom. Others felt that there was little the US could or should do about the changing attitudes of many people in countries volunteering to go communist. Left-wing commentators felt that communism was an attractive doctrine in its own right, and that it was wrong to try to stop it by military means. Conservatives felt there was a great deal of duress, manipulation and military persuasion being used to spread the communist message and therefore felt that it was an appropriate use of American weapons to confront the communist menace. There was never any question of the United Nations seeking to prevent communist subversion of states. With two communist states on the Security Council no one ever thought it likely that the United Nations would take such action. The United

Nations also saw that given the disagreement in senior Western circles over the extent to which the conversion to communism was a voluntary process, it would have been hazardous in the extreme to introduce any United Nations force into such a situation.

The Cold War tested US resolve and encouraged its presidents and a sometimes difficult Congress to spend extremely large sums of money on fashioning the US arsenal, keeping it in working order and improving the technology. The shock to the US psyche when the Soviet communists caught up with the atomic and hydrogen bombs was considerable. There was an even bigger shock to the psyche when Russia leapfrogged the US in the space race and put the first man into orbit. Defeat in Vietnam, despite the superiority of weaponry, caused great disputes within US politics. The US fought back. Where the late 1950s and early 1960s were tense, by the 1970s and 1980s the US lead was growing with surprising speed. Looking back at the technological race, it appears that the communist system was capable of matching heavy industry, basic atomic technology and the technology of the wireless resistor cathode and electrical equipment. The communist world proved quite incapable of matching the supremacy of US technology based upon the silicon chip, the computer, new materials and stealth design. By the early 1990s, US weapons were supreme. Wherever they were tested in open warfare against Russian-supplied equipment, even where that Russian-supplied equipment was well backed up with technical support, the US arms triumphed easily.

It was partly the clear establishment of US supremacy reinforced by President Reagan's Star Wars programme, a missile protection system which would have completely changed the balance of terror, that led to the collapse of communism in the early 1990s. Far-sighted communists like President Gorbachev in the Soviet Union realised that the game was up. They realised that their economic and social system was failing to deliver the breakthroughs, the technical leaps, the more open working which enabled the US systems to excel. The collapse of communism in all parts of the world, save China and Cuba, led to but a short period of rejoicing in the West. Instead of removing the imminent threat of nuclear war, the lifting of the Iron Curtain in Europe and the breakdown of the Communist bloc, opened up old wounds and divides between nations, races and ideologies. It led directly to the collapse of Yugoslavia, the separation of Czechoslovakia, old arguments about the true borders of Hungary and Poland, and an uneasy relationship between the Baltic States and the former Soviet Union.

Local wars characterised the experiences in Latin America, in Asia, in Africa and in the Middle East. The last 50 years have seen frequent flare-ups between the Arabs and the Israelis. Chile has fought Argentina, Iraq has made its bid for supremacy in the Arab world, China has threatened Taiwan, and Japan has had an uneasy relationship with its giant neighbour. At times, the US – acting through the UN or on its own – has been decisive in avoiding conflict. There have been several occasions when the US has imposed its will or its ships to ensure that Taiwan has not been invaded by China. US diplomacy and sometimes force of arms has been important in keeping an uneasy peace over many years in the Middle East. No one around the world is likely to make a move of any military significance without first asking the question, 'What might the US do if we did this?'

It is perhaps easier for Britain to understand the awesome responsibilities and the feelings subsequently generated in the US because Britain was the world's previous superpower. In the nineteenth century it was the British Navy that was the force to be reckoned with. Larger than any other two navies that could be assembled against it, the British Navy straddled the world with bases and ports of arrival and departure on shores of the five continents. It was Britain who often took the lead in sorting out conflicts in the Middle East, in trying to force China into more Western ways, interfering in the futures of the fledgeling Latin American republics, fighting in the Crimea against the Russians, or attempting to exercise its influence on the continent of Europe when tensions flared up between France, Germany and the other great powers. This experience lives on in the folk memory. It means the British people have more natural sympathy with the US dilemma of whether to intervene or to leave well alone, and more understanding of how the rest of the world can retaliate.

The global vocation of the US

Twentieth-century US policy has been characterised by many arguments. One of the most critical has been whether the US should withdraw into its continental frontiers or whether it should continue with any kind of world role. There have been periods when the isolationists have held sway. The US was very reluctant to commit forces in either the First or Second World War. The US did not enter the First World War until 1917, and then only when it thought Germany might foment trouble on the Mexican border. If Japan had not struck at Pearl Harbor in 1941, the US would not have entered the conflict as a combatant. If Germany had not declared war on the US it may have remained reluctant to declare war on Germany. Sitting in the Midwest or on the Californian seaboard, it is very easy for US citizens to say, 'What are those faraway conflicts in Europe to do with us?' Whilst many US people can trace their descent to Italians or Spaniards, British or Irish, it does not necessarily mean that they share the views of the successive generations who have remained in the old countries who have yet again fallen out with each other. The US is a great melting pot which has brought together these different races, languages and cultures and fashioned out of them one mighty country. Irish, British, Spanish and Italian Americans are more likely to see eye to eye in favouring non-intervention in a European war than they are to return to the old battles re-enacted over there. It has so often been events which have impelled the US to intervene in Europe, rather than any more elevated sense of duty.

In recent years the US has become impatient about the lack of progress to a more integrated Europe. Successive presidential teams have thought it would be convenient to have one Europe, one unified command, one larger country that they could do business with. Successive administrations have hoped that Germany would start to spend more on weaponry itself and take more of an interest in the wider world around. Many Americans have been urging Germany to overturn the *Grundgesetz* or basic law adopted by Germany at the end of the Second World War on the advice of the Allied powers. This constitutional document expressly forbade German troops to be deployed outside the country's own borders. Many have felt that the Germans and other European countries have been free-riding on the back of the US taxpayers' generosity, deliberately spending far less European national product on defence, safe in the knowledge that they were covered by the US nuclear and conventional weapons umbrella.

There has also been a strong revisionist strand, particularly in Republican thinking, as events have unfolded. The decision of the German government to do a deal with Russia about Russian troops in East Germany without first consulting the US properly caused considerable alarm in Washington after the rapid reunification of the two Germanies. The realisation that Germany was going to follow an *ostpolitik* of its own, trying to bring Hungary, Poland, the Czech Republic and Slovakia into a European federation which could do business direct with Moscow, worried the US, which still sees Moscow as the most important second-power centre on the planet, and the one that needs to be viewed with the greatest suspicion. When this has been allied to a number of positions adopted by the EU which are seen by the US as unhelpful, maybe in restraint of trade, or against other US interests, it provides a reason for caution in US policy circles over the idea of a United Europe.

So how then is the *Pax Americana* likely to develop? We can make certain forecasts. For the foreseeable future, it is highly likely that US military dominance will survive. Indeed, such is the speed of the digital revolution in the US, and such are the relative levels of defence spending, that we may witness a further increase in the lead as US technology and defence spending outstrips those of any other country or group of countries. It is inconceivable that Moscow could quickly regain first-power status, given the enfeebled state of the former Soviet economy and the growing internal problems within the rather ramshackle Russian Federation. It looks extremely unlikely that electorates and governments in the EU are going to make a sea change in the amount they spend on defence. Many of the leading continental countries are also finding it difficult to keep up or catch up with the US lead in digital technology. The US defence industry simply outclasses the more disparate European one in terms of its capacity for innovation, long production runs and commercial success.

We are therefore going to continue to live in a world where the US will be able to call the shots. No country around the world is going to wish to push the US over the edge, to test the giant's patience too much, given the colossal superiority of its missile systems, its military planes, the size of its navy, and its capacity to mobilise huge numbers of well armed troops.

Life at the top can be tough

However, the giant also has a vulnerable side. We are going to live in a world where more and more countries have access to basic nuclear technology, and where many countries follow in the path of Iraq by developing the capability to engage in chemical and biological warfare. Chemical, biological and nuclear warfare is difficult to counter for a democracy which does not wish to place the lives of its troops or its civilian population in jeopardy. The US has lived through a relatively long period when, with the exception of the Soviet Union, no one was able to threaten the mainland of the US. China, or Middle Eastern tyrannies, did not have rockets with sufficient range to target New York City or Washington, DC. No one felt that any country in Europe, the Middle East or Asia could unleash naval or air forces that were likely to survive the barrage of US firepower clustered offshore and in defensive locations throughout the US. The Russians became petrified when the US looked as if it was close to designing an anti-missile system which would have made redundant Russia's threat of striking from afar through unmanned rockets.

The world has also noticed that US democracy is particularly open, that its people are understandably reluctant to sacrifice any part of their luxurious lifestyle and will ask lots of questions before allowing their president, their Commander-in-Chief, to commit US troops to dangerous situations. The biggest threat to US power in the short to medium term is the actions of dedicated groups of terrorists, guerrilla bands and those who are prepared to use weapons that the West has banned to blackmail and terrorise others. This is why the US has been particularly keen to launch missile or bomb attacks on any recalcitrant tyrant who looks as if he is close to making useable quantities of biological or chemical weapons, or may be developing a nuclear capability of his own.

Looking beyond the short to medium term, we cannot take US superiority for granted. Whilst there is nothing yet to suggest that any country is about to challenge US technical superiority, there are several large countries around the world with much bigger populations which could provide a serious threat to democratic institutions and free societies, at least in their parts of the world, if they decided to use their considerable muscle power, conventional weapons or fledgeling nuclear power with less concern for human life than is shown by the Western democracies. The first part of the twenty-first century is likely to continue to see the US as a technical and economic giant backed by the most formidable arsenal of weapons the world has ever seen. As the twenty-first century advances, so people in the US and the other Western democracies will have to adjust to the idea that our societies have relatively small populations and that, in terms of economic power, other parts of the world are catching up or have surpassed us.

The scale of military forces in the EU, the UK and the US

Whilst the effective military strength of the European countries is modest compared with that of the US, we should not underestimate the continental powers either. The US is much stronger in the field of bombers, naval power and missiles. It has the ability to project and carry its power to every corner of the world, whereas much of the power of the continental military machines is based on land armies capable only of conventional operation on the continent of Europe. Table 3.1 shows, however, that if Britain joined a military alliance with Europe and gradually disengaged with the other countries from NATO, the EU would be a formidable military power in its own right, second only to the US. The EU countries excluding the UK have more combat aircraft than the US. If the UK's bombers were added to the rather small number of other European countries' bombers, then in that field, too, the EU defence arm would have more planes than the US. The EU without the UK already has substantially more military personnel than the US, a supremacy which would be underlined if the UK joined the European defence union.

Table 3.1   **Military Strength**

	Combat Aircraft	Bombers	Military personnel
US	2,398	206	1,443,600
EU ex UK	2,596	45	2,057,140
UK	284	175	208,600
US + UK	2,682	381	1,652,200
EU + UK	2,880	220	2,265,740

	Aircraft Carriers	Cruisers/ destroyers	Frigates	Submarines
US	12	86	40	84
EU ex UK	4	21	128	72
UK	3	12	20	12
US + UK	15	98	60	96
EU + UK	7	33	148	84

At sea the US is the dominant nation. Its twelve aircraft carriers surpass even the combined forces of the EU and the UK. Similarly, its number of larger warships, cruisers and destroyers show the US clearly in the lead, even if the UK joined the combined European defence force. EU countries have a large flotilla of frigates and would, if the UK joined them, match in numbers but not in power the submarine force of the US.

The EU forces would be eclipsed by the unmanned long-range capability of US missiles. Recent conflicts have shown the problems the EU forces have. Whilst the EU outnumbers the US in terms of military personnel, it finds it very difficult to concentrate them and carry them to the scene of operation rapidly. It does not have the air support, the heavy lift and the naval flexibility that the US has developed and paid for over the years. The US has decided as an island continent that it needs to shape foreign policy and support it in the five continents and oceans of the world. To do so, it has outpaced all other countries in terms of naval, missile and air force capability. The US not only has a technological lead, it also has more ships and planes to deliver its weaponry to the four corners and five continents of the world.

Britain's decision whether to join the EU defence organisation or to strengthen a transatlantic one is, nonetheless, important. As the figures reveal, the British Navy is an important force. It almost matches the rest of the EU in aircraft carriers and air capability and has an important force of cruisers, destroyers and frigates which are well armed by European standards. The UK bomber force is an important strategic branch of the West's aerial capability; and the British Army, whilst small, is famed for its professionalism, its high standards of training and its ability to deploy in very difficult conditions. This is why the current debates about whether the UK should submerge itself in a European defence union or should be the strongest voice in Europe for a stronger NATO is crucial. Whilst no one is suggesting that the EU would have immediate hostile military intent against the US, nor is anyone suggesting that it would have the missile, naval or aerial capability to launch any attack, it would be a more uncomfortable feeling for the US if the united European forces, including the UK, developed along the lines that some are suggesting.

The special relationship

More than half a century later, and we are still living in the long shadow cast by the Second World War. The only reason Germany and Japan are not today colossal nuclear and military powers is that they were deliberately disarmed by the Allies at the end of the Second World War and have been circumspect about the extent of their rearmament ever since. I remember visiting Berlin just before the Wall came down. I still have in my possession one of the last passes of the British military government for the British sector of Berlin, issued to a British visitor. Although it was only a decade ago, it could have been a different age. Berlin was partitioned. It remained under military government and people could only come out and go across the wall and between the sectors if they had the necessary paperwork. The fall of the Berlin Wall changed a great deal, but much of the rest of the post-war architecture has remained in place. Germany and Japan are not members of the UN Security Council. They are not nuclear powers. Their technical development in the latter part of the twentieth century has been much more heavily directed towards civil uses than military ones, leaving the field free for the US and, to a lesser extent, Britain and France. At the end of the Second World War the US in particular attracted a great deal of the German technical and weapons-making talent to the great research laboratories in the western continent, and made good use of the expertise they had acquired. Whilst Europe was attempting to overcome the problems of poverty, mass migration and endless bomb sites, the US, safe in its continental redoubt, was getting on with the business of making sure it had the superpower weaponry for the second half of the twentieth century.

Why, then, given US superiority, has it been seemingly so keen to have Britain as an ally? When the war ended, Britain was a serious partner. It was after all the UK that had kept the conflict going in the dog days of 1940 and 1941 before the US entered the war and geared up to take it seriously. It was above all Churchill's voice and tones which rang in the ears of many Americans, making them realise that freedom was on the line, and that Britain was prepared to put in a super-human effort. Whilst the US could see that Britain had given a great deal, was poor, was overstretching its resources, and was going to be the junior partner in the final attack upon Hitler's continental fortress, it could also see that Britain was a critical partner, carrying more than its fair share of the burden of defending the West when compared with its means. This naturally earned Britain considerable respect, aided by the way Churchill determined to play the part of one of the big three wartime leaders in all the important conferences and meetings. It may have been a US general who led the victorious Allied forces into Germany, but no one doubted the role played by the RAF, by the British Army in Burma, by Montgomery in the desert, by the British Army that had fought its way up through Italy or by the excellent British forces which had landed on their own D-Day beaches and made their way to Berlin itself. The Union flag could proudly fly alongside the Stars and Stripes as a serious partner.

There is, however, little sentiment in relationships even between friends and allies in the international arena. The US clearly saw that by the end of the war it was its mighty industrial and war machine that had proved decisive. Looking ahead, the US saw that it was going to be its money, the scientific base, its ability to use wandering German and even British talent, and its ability to extend its lead technically and economically that would make it the dominant power of the latter twentieth century. The British sometimes suffered from an inferiority complex which they concealed well to US minds who felt that Britain came across often as pompous and superior. The use of Britain as a wartime base camp for the US forces that were to invade the continent of Europe had not always helped relations. For every GI marriage, there were another two or three people who had formed bad impressions on both sides. The British resented the Americans' easy access to wealth and success. The Americans were somewhat scornful of a little, old, tired, dirty country, as they saw it, peeking out from behind the blackout sheets and muddling through with the ration books.

Successive British prime ministers decided that the best way of keeping Britain alive and sitting around the big table was to remain a special friend of the US. Churchill set it off with the ringing declarations of English-Speaking Union in his Fulton, Missouri, speech. It was continued, especially by Harold Macmillan, who was determined that Britain should have access to the best of US weapons technology; by Harold Wilson, who even flirted with the idea of a US union himself; by James Callaghan, and quintessentially by Margaret Thatcher with her very special political relationship with her friend Ronald Reagan.

It was easy to see what the UK was getting out of this. Britain could enjoy some of the reflected strength and glory of the US position. Britain could gain from joint deals and the sharing of technology with the US defence industry. Britain could help the US intervene well beyond Britain's own capacity to intervene separately and on its own.

The policy, however, did have its drawbacks from the British point of view. Perhaps the worst reversal came at the time of Suez. Britain still felt it had the power and authority to intervene with France in an area that affected one of its crucial interests. Britain had always been the titan of the Middle East. It was the British and French who had seen through the Suez Canal in the first place. It was British shipping lines more than any others which were thought to be at risk. The failure of the US to back the British action and the climbdown which followed caused resentments on this side of the Atlantic but also summed up the *realpolitik* of the power balance. From Suez onwards, Britain was unable to go it alone if the US disagreed with its actions.

More recently, Britain had to finesse the US relationship when it decided to intervene to recapture the Falklands. In the end, US intelligence and support behind the scenes was helpful, but there were some difficult times when the British government was not entirely sure that Washington would approve of all it was doing and was well aware that if Washington turned against the operation – at best hazardous – it would become impossible. It is never easy for a former imperial power that once bestrode the world like a colossus itself to accept the dominance of another nation, especially one that had spun off following an open rebellion against the mother country.

But what was there in this relationship for the US? It is important not to underestimate the loneliness of the world's only superpower. Whilst the US knows that it has the military might to do more or less what it wishes, being a democracy it also knows that it has to behave to high standards and that there are moral and political pressures constraining its action, as well as military ones. The US could successfully invade virtually any country on the planet and take the country over if it was so minded, and if it was prepared to accept the retaliation, the hatred and the loss of life that would entail. Because the US is a freedom-loving democracy which practises what it preaches on the self-determination of peoples, this has never crossed policy-makers' minds as an option in Washington. It is this type of consideration that has often meant to Washington that London has a use. It is good when advancing a strong case in the councils of the world for Washington to be able to say that it is not alone in taking this view. Britain, too, has considerable moral authority in the world. Whilst there are still those who resent some elements of colonial experience or who resent the side Britain may have taken in some long-forgotten war, there are many others around the world who have valued British involvement on the side of freedom and self-determination against the abuse of power or tyranny. There are many in former colonies who now, freed of British control, recognise that Britain did bequeath some good things from that colonial experience. There are traditions of democratic practice, fair play, sound administration and honest dealing which have served many a former colonial country rather better than some of the bad habits or traditions picked up in other parts of the world. So the US has been able to draw on that reservoir of contacts, goodwill, skill and diplomatic understanding that Britain at its best has been able to demonstrate.

There have been times when British military support has also been valuable. In the earlier part of the post-war period Britain still had a large number of important and well located bases which could add to the strength of the joint position. Although Britain now has very modest armaments in terms of numbers compared with the US, Britain's armaments are among some of the most modern and effective in the world, and the adjunct of British expertise, British ships, British aeroplanes or British missiles alongside US ones can be a useful addition. The US may have the high-level Stealth bombers, but Britain, for example, has the Harrier jump jets. British know-how and military capability can also be valuable. Britain fought a different pattern of wars to the US in the twentieth century, whilst at the same time fighting many of the big ones alongside the US itself. Britain learned a great deal about jungle warfare in Burma, about amphibious landing capability in the Falklands theatre, about policing tense and difficult situations in Northern Ireland: these things are of use to the US and there has been some joint training and debriefing.

We should not underestimate the importance of the common language and the interests of the personalities involved. Many British prime ministers have enjoyed hobnobbing with US presidents. US presidents, often short of language skills themselves, have rather welcomed being able to meet largely friendly foreign leaders who speak their own language and enjoy some of the same pursuits. The common culture, language and history has often helped and has meant that it is very likely that a US president is going to get on better with a British prime minister, and vice versa, than with a prime minister from Japan or a chancellor from Germany. The common understanding inherited on both sides of the Atlantic can do wonders for the special relationship.

There are those who now fashionably say that the special relationship is dead. Those in Britain who scorn Britain and the British, who think that we are now already part of a much bigger European empire, try to play down our significance to the US and ridicule the idea that we will any longer be important enough in Washington to warrant that special status. There are those in Washington who still hanker after the big European scheme, who see the special relationship as a bygone relic of the former age. There are other isolationists in Washington who do not want a special relationship with anybody because it may bring with it trouble and the impulse to intervene in world events. There were times in the Thatcher–Reagan relationship when Thatcher was providing the lead as to where the two powers combined should seek to assert their influence. There was the famous moment in the Bush–Thatcher relationship when Thatcher told the president memorably not to wobble in prosecuting the war against Iraq.

It is my judgement that the special relationship will have its ups and downs and there will be times when indeed forces on either side of the Atlantic will conspire to suggest it is over. But it is also my judgement that it is not over, because the language, culture and common history still count for a certain amount; history is likely to throw up new pairs of presidents and prime ministers who actually like each other; and there is still logic on both sides to carry on trying to make something of the common defence arrangements. It is true that there are now strong pressures to have a common European defence industry in opposition to that of the US. There are those who would like to do in defence what Airbus has done in the civil aviation sphere, creating a rival to the US and encouraging some kind of trade and technical war between the two. It is true that there is now much more common European defence procurement and a British prime minister who has boasted of a special relationship with the president is at the same time busily trying to rush us into a special defence arrangement with our European partners.

Nonetheless, as the twenty-first century opens, it still remains a perfectly viable option for Britain to develop a special relationship across the Atlantic, to build a bigger common defence industry across the Atlantic, to pool more know-how and to make common cause. Naturally, Britain will have to give more than it takes when it comes to deciding the common policy, because the US is making the bigger contribution. The reality is also that if Britain gave up trying to influence the US, it would not stop the US from dominating the world. Britain would have traded its sometimes significant influence with the world's superpower for an attempt to provide a challenge from European sources that is unlikely to work. It would be better for Britain to recognise this, and to accept that the defence of our freedom rests upon that special relationship across the Atlantic as surely as it has done for more than sixty years. No one could be sure that we would have won without US involvement in the Second World War. What we can be sure of is that Western Europe would have been under threat from communist forces if the US nuclear umbrella had not been hastily erected to prevent such a disaster in the 1950s and 1960s.

4
Free Trade and Democracy: The Ideals of the Wider English-Speaking Commonwealth

The United Nations was not the only body to be established after 1945 to try to make the world a safer and better place. As the victor powers surveyed the rubble of the civilisation which had given its all to war, they tried to embody in a new global architecture the values they held dear. Both the US and the UK value liberty. British history is based on the story of the struggle to limit the actions of the king, to gain the vote, and to mobilise public opinion. The US nation was born from the Boston Tea Party, asserting the right to settle their own affairs in a democratic manner. Whereas Germany and Italy had struggled to unite their countries and were used to strong central power, whereas the smaller European countries were more worried about external threats to their freedom than internal ones, the two Anglo-Saxon countries saw the world in terms of trying to secure traditional democratic freedoms.

In the post-Second World War world, a number of important international institutions and agreements were established to supplement the UN. There was a new financial settlement. Out of the ruins of continental Europe and Asia grew a new global settlement. The idea was to increase progress towards free trade, the free movement of people and capital, and to make money available to countries in need of redevelopment and reconstruction. The leading world organisa-tions of the post 1945 period and the EU went about their tasks of gaining international agreement and promoting common action in very different ways. The major world institutions respected national sovereignty rather more and have proved surprisingly flexible and durable. They have not always been effective because they require agreement to proceed. In contrast, the EU is now moving into a position where it does not respect the interests and views of individual member states and is proving less flexible.

WTO and GATT

One of the most visionary institutions was the General Agreement on Tariffs and Trade (GATT) established in 1947 and still with us in revised form as the World Trade Organization (WTO) today. Australia, Belgium, Brazil, Burma, Canada, Ceylon, Chile, China, Cuba, Czechoslovakia, France, India, Lebanon, Luxembourg, the Netherlands, New Zealand, Norway, Pakistan, Southern Rhodesia, Syria, South Africa, the UK and the US came together to raise standards of living and ensure full employment through more open trade. They agreed to a substantial reduction of tariffs and other barriers and the elimination of discriminatory treatment in interna-tional commerce. The first article of the Agreement set out a general most-favoured nation treatment. The exports of any signatory country should attract the same favourable terms as the exports to that country from any other territory. The only exceptions were if a charge was equivalent to an internal tax imposed on domestic product, or an anti-dumping duty permitted under Article 6 of the Treaty. Clause 3 of the Treaty bans the imposition of discriminatory taxes upon imported products. Similarly, any law or regulation relating to the product should not penalise the import compared with domestically produced goods.

Countries were allowed to impose screen quotas on imported films for the cinema, as countries were especially sensitive about this issue in the early days of GATT. Goods are guaranteed freedom of transit throughout the territory of each contracting party. No discrimination was permitted based on the flag of the vessel, or the place of origin, departure, entry, exit or destination of the goods. Nor was the contracting party allowed to hold the goods up unreasonably at customs points. Imported goods had to be fairly valued for customs purposes to avoid any hidden additional imposition. Fees and charges related to import and export should be realistic in relation to the actual costs incurred. Quotas, import and export licences and other quantitative restrictions were banned under Article 11. There was some leeway in the situation where there was a run on the currency and difficulties with the balance of payments in any individual country's case. Where special measures had to be introduced, the other countries were given rights to enter into discussion over the reasonableness of these measures. Article 15 established that the contracting parties to GATT would also cooperate with the International Monetary Fund (IMF). Indeed, the GATT agreement stresses in several places that where the IMF is pursuing a policy to help a given country then compatible action may be taken under GATT to try to return the country to stability and equilibrium on balance of payments and its monetary account. The architecture of the post-war financial world had been carefully constructed to ensure compatibility between the main arms of world jurisdiction. Article 16 attempted to restrict countries' subsidies at home, where these helped undercut imports from abroad. Article 17 recognised the especial threat to free trade posed by state trading enterprises and tried to limit it.

A number of general exceptions are written into Article 20 of the Treaty. Governments were allowed to take action to protect public morals; to protect human, animal or plant life or health; to control the importation or exportation of gold and silver; to ensure customs enforcement; to allow the products of prison labour to be protected; to protect national treasures for artistic, historic or archaeological purposes; to conserve exhaustible natural resources, and to stabilise certain markets. Countries were also allowed to keep information back for security purposes. These wide-ranging exemptions showed just how fearsome the contracting states were, particularly at the beginning of the GATT process. Many of them did feel that freer trade was bad news for them rather than good, or that the costs of international specialisation were going to be very substantial in terms of lost jobs and closed industries.

Each nation signing the original Treaty was given one vote at all meetings. The Secretary-General of the UN had to convene the first meeting of contracting parties in 1948. Article 28 revealed that GATT was going to be a continuous process, setting out the need for further rounds of tariff negotiations to reduce them gradually over time. Article 36 recognised the need to link greater access for the developing countries to the more advanced countries' markets, with suitable lending from the international institutions to encourage more rapid trade and economic development.

The World Trade Organization

GATT grew to enjoy a much larger list of countries. In 1994 they decided to establish the World Trade Organization (WTO). This new agreement confirmed that the principal objective of GATT and its replacement organisation, the WTO, was to raise standards of living and ensure full employment. This was to be achieved as the original GATT signatories envisaged, by steadily growing trade between them. In 1994 the countries added the objective of sustainable development, seeking to protect and preserve the environment. They continued to recognise that the countries were at different levels of economic development with different needs. The countries 'resolved to develop an integrated, more viable and durable multilateral trading system, encompassing the General Agreement on Tariffs and Trade, the results of past trade liberalisation efforts, and all of the results of the Uruguay round of multilateral trade negotiations'. Article 1 established the World Trade Organization. The new WTO was designed to provide a forum for negotiations amongst the members and a way of ensuring that the decisions were followed through. A dispute settlement procedure was established, and a trade policy review mechanism put in place. The WTO is required to cooperate with the IMF and with the International Bank for Reconstruction and Development (IBRD) as the predecessor GATT Treaty had sketched.

The WTO has a Ministerial Conference composed of representatives of all the members, meeting at least once every two years. In between ministerial conferences, a General Council, including representatives of all the member states, is available to meet and to conduct business. The General Council can review both disputes and general trade policy. Under its guidance a separate Council for Trade and Goods, a Council for Trade and Services, and a Council for Trade Related Aspects of Intellectual Property Rights was established. The Ministerial Conference established a Committee on Trade and Development, a Committee on Balance of Payments Restrictions, and a Committee on Budget, Finance and Administration. Special attention was paid to arrangements for helping lesser developed countries to catch up with other members. A Director-General is responsible for presenting an annual budget and for ensuring that members pay their dues to maintain the administrative structure. Consensus decision-making is still favoured, but arrangements are in place to enable votes to occur with each member state continuing to have one vote as originally decided in 1947.

The 1994 Agreement contained a large number of annexes. The first general one urged member states to notify where they had state trading enterprises that could be an obstacle to free and fair trade, to set out schemes for getting rid of restrictions imposed on trade for balance of payments reasons, and reviewed customs unions to try to ensure that they too were compliant with GATT. Agriculture is an area of particular difficulty as all parts of the world have protective and subsidised regimes. In this agreement the members reaffirmed their belief that we need 'a fair and market-orienting agriculture trading system'. In a valiant attempt to begin to combat the grotesque distortions of the agricultural market the governments set out a schedule limiting subsidies. Given the lack of substantial agreement on these measures, a number of loopholes were permitted, including the need for regional assistance and for environmental intervention.

The Agreement on Sanitary and Phyto-Sanitary Measures attempted to limit the damage that individual member states could cause by claiming a restriction is needed to protect human or animal life. The member states decided that they needed to move towards a more harmonised system of assessing risk and taking trade action. The Annex on Textile Products attempted to bring them more fully into the spirit and letter of the general world trade agreements. A special agreement attempted to ensure that technical regulations were not being prepared with a view to discriminating against imported products. If possible, member states should use international standards when drawing up technical regulations.

Dumping

Member states came up with a revised definition of dumping.

> A product is considered as being dumped, i.e., introduced into the commerce of another country at less than its normal value, if the export price of the product exported from one country to another

is less than the comparable price, in the ordinary course of trade, for the like product when destined for consumption in the exporting country.

If no such comparison is possible, then the cost of production is taken into account plus a reasonable amount for administrative selling and general costs and for profits.

New Articles set out a strong method for investigating when allegations of dumping are received, including full investigation of the industrial background against which the alleged dumping has taken place. All those who are party to the dispute will be invited to provide detailed information so that the authorities can come to a sensible conclusion. If dumping is discovered, then the problem can be remedied – either by the manufacturer putting up the prices for export, or by the imposition of an anti-dumping duty. The WTO set out rules concerning pre-shipment inspection so that an importing country could satisfy itself before the consignment was shipped that it met with the necessary rules and regulations. The WTO also set out guidelines controlling rules of origin for the labelling of products. The WTO now bans subsidies which are contingent upon export performance and subsidies which prefer the use of domestic over imported goods. If a member state persists with such a subsidy the WTO has the power to demand its withdrawal.

Fair trade in services

In 1994 a breakthrough was made in extending the GATT treatment from goods to trade in services as well. The opening preamble to the agreement on trade and services saw growing trade in services as an important means of promoting economic growth and greater development. Promoting a fair trade in services is, by its nature, much more difficult, with the added problem of the huge regulatory involvement of government in service provision. The early WTO attacks on unfair treatment included recognising that technical standards and licensing requirements could be a significant barrier to service trade across frontiers. Where a member state recognises the educational qualifications or experience attained in another country, it should be prepared to offer similar recognition to other interested members. The intention is to move towards multilateral recognition, otherwise it is impossible for people to provide services like accountancy and legal advice across frontiers.

The WTO recognises that in a number of service areas monopolies have been established by trade bodies, professional associations or member states. The WTO is moving towards breaking such monopolies. A process has been set up reminiscent of that in the post-war period to liberalise trade in goods. Regular five-yearly rounds of trade liberalisation in services are to be held, progressively reducing the number of tariff and non-tariff barriers that stand in the way of the free exchange of services across frontiers.

Intellectual property rights

The agreement on trade-related intellectual property rights states: 'each member should accord to the nationals of other member states treatment no less favourable than it accords to its own nationals with regard to the protection of intellectual property'. Once any protection is given to an intellectual property in favour of companies from one country, the member state has to offer the same protection to companies from other countries. Much of the agreement on intellectual property is restrictive rather than enabling. For example, it allows protection of trademarks and protection of copyright for at least 50 years. Industrial designs that are protected are accorded ten years' protection. Patents are also reserved subject to suitable safeguards.

The defence of trademarks, intellectual property, design and new formulations has caused considerable tension in the debates between the poor and the richer world. The advanced world has considerable weight in trade matters, reflecting its economic strength and the importance of its trade flows. These countries are very keen on the protection of brands, designs and patents because most of them are developed in advanced Western countries. Developing countries struggling to get on in the world often see these protections as getting in their way. It means they have to pay licensing or royalty revenues to the first world countries in order to catch up with their technology and ideas.

In order to encourage fair and free trade the GATT rules attempt to distinguish between the defence of a competitive advantage which an individual entrepreneur, innovator, or company has achieved, on the one hand, and allowing the free exploitation of general design features and general processes which advance world prosperity, on the other. The dividing line is not an easy one to draw and as a result there have been endless trade battles, often pitting the first world against the third world. In recent years the pace of technical innovation in the computing world has produced two different types of problem. It becomes increasingly difficult to defend any intellectual property as the design and discovery cycles are now so short. There has been an explosion of new companies exploiting ideas that bear a strong family resemblance. On the other hand, the incredible success of Microsoft in forming the software platform for most new PC computer applications has led the US Anti-Trust authorities to attempt to limit this dominant company which has emerged directly from the pressures of the marketplace.

The Commonwealth

The Commonwealth currently has 53 countries with a population of over 1500 million. It began as a collection of states that had been colonies and dominions of the British Empire, led by the United Kingdom alongside Australia, Canada and South Africa. Many states joined the Commonwealth when they were liberated from British colonial rule, especially in Africa in the 1960s. Now unconnected states like Mozambique have also joined. The queue of states seeking admission believe that the unique combination of respect for their sovereignty but greater influence when needed in international negotiations is a desirable one for them. The present requirement to join seems to be a combination of a democratic system, a reasonable record on human rights and some commitment to the English language. The Commonwealth has become an especially good platform for African states in a world increasingly ignoring the whole continent. France has formed a similar but lesser grouping for the francophone countries.

The Commonwealth provides us with an example of the type of structure more suited to the dot.com free-flowing world of the twenty-first century than the tight central controls of the EU. The Commonwealth structure is based on an unwritten set of procedures, not on a formal constitution or code. It is a voluntary association of states where each country remains responsible for its own policies. The role of the Commonwealth is to have clout where the members agree to act in the common interest together. The Commonwealth is not attempting to pick power struggles with the UN, the US or NATO. It respects other world associations and attempts to work with them and through them as well as on its own. Whilst there is no codified statute setting up the Commonwealth, we do have the Declaration of Commonwealth Principles set out at the summit in Singapore in 1971. The Declaration stresses the importance of it being a voluntary association of independent sovereign states coming from territories all over the world at very different stages of development. The Commonwealth brings together a rich variety of cultures, traditions and institutions and allows a member to be non-aligned, or to belong to any other military or trade grouping, association or alliance. What the Commonwealth member states hold in common is a set of principles. They come together because they wish to influence international society for the benefit of mankind.

Like the UN, the Commonwealth is established to maintain international peace and order and to promote security and prosperity. The Commonwealth believes 'in the liberty of the individual, in equal rights for all citizens regardless of race, colour, creed, or political belief, and in their inalienable right to participate by means of free and democratic political processes in framing the society in which they live'. Personal freedom under the law is a common heritage and a necessary precondition for membership. As it brings together so many different races, an attack upon racial prejudice is a crucial central tenet. South Africa was expelled from the Commonwealth for its apartheid policy and only readmitted when it had decided to rejoin the civilised world by giving people of all races and colours in South Africa equal political rights.

The Commonwealth is against wide disparities in wealth and seeks 'to overcome poverty, ignorance and disease, in raising standards of life and achieving a more equitable international society'. One of the main ways of achieving this is seen by Commonwealth members as increased free flow of international trade, based on fair exchange. The Commonwealth also acts a conduit for government and private investment monies to be routed from the richer to the poorer areas.

The members of the Commonwealth see themselves as exemplars of a new way of doing business. They 'provide a constructive example of the multinational approach which is vital to peace and progress in the modern world'. The style of business is 'based on consultation, discussion and co-operation'.

The Lusaka Declaration

The anti-racism parts of the Commonwealth's purposes were strengthened in the Lusaka Declaration made in Zambia in 1979. This declaration states that the peoples of the Commonwealth 'have the right to live freely in dignity and equality, without any distinction or exclusion based on race, colour, sex, descent, or national ethnic origin'. No one has the right to perpetuate racial prejudice or discrimination, everyone has the right to equality before the law and unites in condemning apartheid. The Commonwealth sees the need to eliminate racial prejudice not just by legislation, but also public information and education.

The Harare Statement

In Zimbabwe in 1991 the Commonwealth updated its Declaration of General Principles in the Harare Statement. Again, they reaffirmed a belief in the need for a voluntary association of sovereign independent states, each responsible for its own policies. It draws attention to the strength that comes from the diversity of members sharing an inheritance in language, culture and the rule of law, but disagreeing on many other things. The Commonwealth way is 'to seek consensus through consultation and the sharing of experience. It is uniquely placed to serve as a model and as a catalyst for new forms of friendship and co-operation to all in the spirit of the Charter of the United Nations.' The Commonwealth welcomes the end of the Cold War and the growth of democracy and justice. The Commonwealth wants to do more to strengthen and spread democracy and democratic processes, to stand up for fundamental human rights and equalities, to provide universal access to education and to do much more to promote sustainable development. The Commonwealth began to see the need for it to do more to encourage the free flow of multilateral trade, aid and investment. Modern interests were reflected in a statement on the need to protect the environment, to combat drug-trafficking and provide help for the smaller countries to deal with their particular problems. Again, the Commonwealth is aware of the importance of the 'shared historical, professional, cultural and linguistic heritage'.

The Millbrook Action Programme

In New Zealand in 1995, the Commonwealth heads of government set out the Millbrook Action Programme to implement the principles of the previous declarations. The Commonwealth decided it needed to provide assistance in constitutional and legal matters and in the electoral field. The Commonwealth is capable of offering advice on strengthening or developing democracies, on electoral machinery, on civic and voter education and provides observers to ensure fair play at elections. The Commonwealth also pledged itself to take early and strong action in relation to the violation of the Harare Declaration by any country. If a country suffers a coup against a democratically elected government then the Secretary-General of the Commonwealth is to express immediate public disapproval. Negotiations follow to try to ensure an early restoration of democracy. If necessary the country is excluded from participation at ministerial level meetings of the Commonwealth. This can be followed by suspension of attendance at any Commonwealth meeting and the ending of Commonwealth technical assistance. Finally, sanctions and suspension from the Commonwealth can be introduced for persistent offenders.

In order to promote social and economic progress the Commonwealth has decided to promote a greater flow of investment through the Commonwealth Private Investment Initiative, to work for continued progress in reducing debts in an initiative led by the British Chancellor of the Exchequer, to offer assistance in developing self-help schemes and measures to help small and developing states.

The Commonwealth has been busily reinventing itself, as many organisations have had to do against the background of the hurly-burly of globalisation. Where once the Commonwealth was seen as a backward-looking old boys' club, it is now seen as a new kind of trans-governmentalism. As David Howell, one of its protagonists and commentators, has said:

> citizens of the liberal democracies will certainly want many of the globe's problems to be tackled by common action, but they will not tolerate dictation or regulation by unelected officials and remote regulators. The strong preference will be for networks and associations between the agencies of government, as well as

between unofficial and voluntary groupings, to engage in a common enterprise. (Howell 1998)

Howell sees the Commonwealth as working in precisely this way. It can strengthen an independent small sovereign state in the international system when it makes a common cause, but the state is not forced to accept the common cause against its will.

This open, more modern, global organisation that is now forming does have to work closely with the UN, the IMF and the WTO. The signatory states agree that the promotion of open trading offers them the best hope of greater prosperity. They agree that democracy is the best guarantor of their freedoms and that they need collectively a stronger voice in the UN and with the IMF and WTO. There are regular meetings of heads of government supplemented by ministerial and official working parties at all levels. The Commonwealth works by the direct exchange of experience, helped by common traditions solving some common problems. The Commonwealth does not operate by having a large budget of its own. When money is needed the Commonwealth is usually a spur or a stimulus to finding private sector or government-to-government solutions.

The Commonwealth is strengthened by holding a four-yearly Commonwealth Games, and an annual Commonwealth Day. The second Monday in each March is reserved for this purpose and is picked up as a theme in schools throughout the Commonwealth countries. The House of Commons Foreign Affairs Committee's extensive report entitled *The Future Role of the Commonwealth* acted as a catalyst to see that it changed from a pyramid, with the UK granting benefits to a sprawling group of recipients, to a system of networks of mutually beneficial relationships where a surprising amount could be achieved through discussion among equals. The more buoyant mood was reflected in establishing 1997 as the UK Year of the Commonwealth. At the Edinburgh meeting in that year the positive agenda was put forward and accepted for encouraging more rapid economic development. Enthusiasm was reinforced when the World Economic Forum of International Competitivity ranked six Commonwealth countries in the first nine in the list of the most internationally competitive economies in the world.

The Edinburgh Declaration

The Edinburgh Declaration supported the expansion of duty-free access for the least developed countries in world trade. It established a trade and investment access facility under the Commonwealth umbrella, to take advantage of globalisation. It drew up an action programme to remove administrative obstacles to trade. It insisted on maintaining open and transparent investment regimes to encourage investment flows across frontiers. It started work for a Commonwealth code of good practice for national policies to promote these private capital flows, and set an objective of halving the proportion of people living in extreme poverty by the year 2015. The Edinburgh conference drew strength from the Commonwealth success in debt relief. Debt relief initiatives launched at Trinidad in 1990 and at Malta in 1994 became established parts of the IMF and World Bank routines. The Commonwealth, sharing in the use of the English language and common legal governmental traditions, also works beyond government through the exchange of ideas and views involving parliamentarians, lawyers, teachers and other technicians. The Commonwealth is particularly good at ensuring that small countries have a voice in the global world.

NATO

The North Atlantic Treaty Organization is another organisation based upon mutual action of sovereign nation states. It implies a more binding commitment in a given field of action on its members than that which relates to the Commonwealth, but it has none of the capacity to overrule, direct, or prosecute its members in the way that the EU has come to do. What strikes any observer of NATO is the stark simplicity of its founding statute, the fixity of purpose that it has pursued ever since its foundation in Washington on 4 April 1949 and the popularity of the organisation as many other countries seek to join for the security which it offers.

NATO was seen as coexisting peacefully and easily within the framework set out by the UN. The opening of the Treaty reaffirms the signatories' faith in 'the purposes and principles of the Charter of the United Nations'. It states how the member states are 'determined to safeguard the freedom, common heritage and civilisation of their peoples, founded on the principles of democracy, individual liberty and the rule of law'. Article 1 of the Treaty itself states how the parties concerned pledge to settle any international dispute in which they are involved by peaceful means consistent with the purposes of the UN. Members of NATO encourage economic collaboration with each other and favour a stable international order. Above all, NATO is a defensive alliance. Its crucial Article is Article 5, which states:

> the parties agree that an armed attack against one or more of them in Europe or North America will be considered an attack against them all and consequently they agree that, if such an armed attack occurs, each of them, can exercise the right of individual or collective self-defence recognised by Article 51 of the Charter of the United Nations, will assist the party or parties so attacked by taking forthwith, individually and in concert with the other parties, such action as it deems necessary including the use of armed force, to restore and maintain the security of the North Atlantic Area.

Any measures taken would be immediately reported to the Security Council and would be terminated when the Security Council takes measures to restore and maintain international peace.

New members may be invited in subject to the consent of all existing members. Any member may leave later after giving due notice of its intention.

In this respect, NATO is very unlike the EU, which offers no easy way out. The purposes of the EU grow by the day and its jurisdiction is constantly being increased. In contrast, NATO has one single-minded purpose which has been held steady throughout the last 50 years. It has been a very successful organisation as NATO members have not been subject to armed attack. Where they have acted together, they have done so in conjunction with the UN for the enforcement of international order and the preservation of the rights of smaller states to self-determination.

Some people claim that NATO involves as big a sacrifice of sovereignty as membership of the EU. This is not so. Membership of NATO does not prevent a member of NATO from using its forces for its own purposes subject to the normal pressures of the UN and inter-national law. It was not NATO forces that brought the Falkland Islands back from Argentinian occupation. Britain was quite capable of mounting the operation on its own, even though its forces were also part of the NATO guarantee. The problem has never arisen of Britain being asked to take action through NATO that it had no wish to take. Were this ever to happen, Britain could instead refuse and give notice of its intention to leave the organisation. In contrast, Britain regularly has to do things under European law that it disagrees with or does not wish to do, and there is a legal structure to ensure that it conforms.

Global solutions for global problems

In the fast-moving, topsy-turvy dot.com world, it is ever more important that global solutions are sought to global problems. Many more problems are becoming global in scale as people, ideas and money move rapidly across national and continental frontiers. The model for effective government is increasingly shifting to global decision-making and global standards, away from national or regional ones. It is for this reason that we need to consider the best models in each field – in the field of general political and military activities, in the field of environmental and social protection, and in the field of economic development and trade in particular.

The New World Order will be Anglo Saxon and democratic. It is the Anglo-Saxon virtues of freedom of expression, self-determination of peoples, one man one vote, freedom of association, of speech and of the press, which are likely to dominate and grow in stature. The 1990s were a remarkable decade for the spread of democracy and freedom worldwide. We saw countless tyrannies in Eastern and central Europe replaced by fledgeling democratic states. We saw popular revolutions in several Asian and Latin American countries. It was a bad decade for communism and for tyranny, and a good decade for the principles of freedom.

It was also a decade when federations and nations fractured on ethnic lines. The massive break-up of the Soviet empire led on to the disintegration of countries like the Russian Federation and Yugoslavia. Just as the British and French empires had withered away in the 1960s and 1970s, so the great communist empires collapsed in the 1990s. The only exception to the trend was in China, with the re-absorption of Hong Kong, and its continuous pressure on Taiwan.

China has also so far proved the biggest exception to the rule that one man one vote, free speech and democracy is the acceptable standard form of government. Whilst it has swept through Eastern Europe and the Soviet Union itself and is now well established in Latin America, Africa and substantial parts of Asia, led by the Commonwealth countries of India and Pakistan, it has so far failed to capture the world's most populous country. It is an interesting question as to whether China can continue to liberalise its economic system, granting people ever greater degrees of economic freedom without triggering, at some point, a demand for greater political freedom and even for greater political self-expression, which could start to fragment China itself. The smaller Asian states have shown a capacity to combine economic freedom with autocratic government, but the 1990s implied that the tide was turning and that democracy was on the march.

For democracy itself is well geared to be the best form of organisation in a dot.com world. New dot.com technology is designed almost to encourage the pressure group, the free political association, the instant focus group – the perfect lobby machine. It will dramatically transform the way Western democracies operate. The decline of the public meeting and even interest in the ballot box itself will be matched by the rise of the instant website group exerting pressure on officials and ministers to move policy in the direction of the lobbyists' choice. Politics will become more interactive, with politicians having to read and listen to the internet chatter as well as using it as a way of setting out their own message.

An autocracy will find it much more difficult to control opinion and association than in the age of the printing press and the public meeting. Autocrats need to prevent dissenting thoughts and dissenting groups. They have been able to do so relatively successfully in some countries under the old technology by banning certain types of public meeting, or by sending people along to the meetings to spy and create an uneasy feeling for anyone wishing to venture too far with dissident thoughts. They have been able to destroy the presses or their product, and control the distribution of leaflets and books as they are bulky physical items requiring shops and deliveries. It is far more difficult to control the flow of information in the internet age. Those who wish to dissent can operate from outside the geographical boundaries of the state concerned. The leaders in exile can, at the press of a button, send messages into millions of homes using video, telephone lines, satellite links and the internet itself. It is possible for a state to develop massive surveillance over internet and phone lines, but it would be rather like trying to hold back the water in a sieve with your fingers. The communist countries in the 1980s were finding it more and more difficult to block free radio transmissions from outside their territories. Restraining the web and the mobile phone is far more difficult.

Nation-to-nation relationships will continue to be problematic. Those who too readily forecast the end of history when the Berlin Wall came down should by now be nursing their wounds as they understand what a cauldron of religious, racial and nationalistic fervour the whole process has unleashed. Pent up frustrations and disagreements from 50 years of communist tyranny come surging through in a host of complex civil wars. It is no easy task imposing order, even when the world has a benign superpower with the predominant position of the US. As conflicts from Vietnam to the former Yugoslavia have shown, only limited use can be made of overwhelming force if the hearts and minds of people have not been won over and if the people on the ground are in fundamental disagreement one with another. Only good government and leadership by local people on behalf of local people can ultimately stop the conflict and bloodshed.

So what, then, should we be looking for in shaping a world order for the twenty-first century that can contain conflict and create the greater happiness for the greatest number? The UN is advancing into its second half-century. It is far from perfect, but it has the advantage of being there, and having reasonable support much of the time from many of its participants. NATO remains a strong force, attracting new members, and capable of doing what it does extremely well. It is better to build on what we have than to start again. The addition of China to the membership of the Security Council at least gives China a window on the world and the West some idea of what China is up to. The UN will have to realise that strength of numbers and force of arms point in the direction of the leading Asian countries playing a bigger role in world affairs, particularly in Asian affairs, as this century advances. As India, Pakistan and China start to flex their muscles with the capacity to raise and sustain huge armies, and now with some nuclear capability, we have to recognise they will have more influence in the world. It will clearly be necessary for the Western powers to maintain their technical lead and to continue to spend substantial sums of money on their own defence capability and their ability to police hot-spots around the world. The US and the UK need good relationships with Asia. The Commonwealth of English-speaking nations provides one easy way of keeping open the lines of communication to help keep the peace.

5
Doing Business the US Way: Is the UK Growing More like the US Day by Day?

Over the last 50 years the links between the US and UK economy have grown ever stronger. Shared language, the aftermath of the Second World War, and the restless pursuit of European markets by Americans led naturally to a surge of US investment in Britain. What has been less noticed but has been equally pronounced has been the way British companies return the compliment. Indeed, British companies have invested more in the US than US companies have invested in Britain. We have now reached the point where half of all the foreign investment in Britain comes from the United States (Table 5.1). Two-fifths of all Britain's investments around the world are in the US. Only a quarter of foreign investment in Britain has come from our EU trading partners, and only a third of our outward investment has gone to other EU states.

When we look at Britain's wealth held overseas, it gives a very different picture of where our true interests lie compared with the crude trade figures showing that we export a large proportion of our manufactured goods to our near neighbours on the continent. Investment is a much more important and longer-lasting relationship than trade. Many British goods counted as exports to the European continent are in practice exports going through the large *entrepôts* of

Rotterdam and Amsterdam, often destined for markets well beyond the shores of Europe itself. When we sell things like oil into the European market, we are selling a commodity product which will sell on price in dollars according to demand. Building investment relationships requires much more understanding, common working and friendship to make it succeed.

Table 5.1 Cumulative inward net investment to the UK 1993–8

		£ million	%
From	US	54,893	53
	Switzerland	16,206	16
	Netherlands	6,659	6
	Germany	4,980	5
	France	4,775	5
	Australia	3,304	3
	Irish Republic	2,274	2
	Belgium/Luxembourg	1,633	2
	Bermuda	1,630	2
	Norway	1,162	1
	Others		5
	(Main EU partners)		20

Source: *Hansard*, House of Lords, 14 February 2000, Answer to Lord Pearson.

There are many reasons why the lure of the US has been much bigger for British companies than the lure of the continent of Europe. Most British businessmen have little or no understanding of French, Spanish, Italian and German. The language barrier is a very considerable one. They can go to New York or Washington, immediately make themselves understood, and establish friendships and investment relationships quite quickly. There is a common culture in the Anglo-Saxon business world drawing on the strength of the common language.

Many British businesses have found it extremely difficult to make money on the continent. Markets are more protected and cartelised. It is more difficult to gain entry into those markets and exceedingly difficult to convert that entry into profitability. Many great British retailers have sought their fortune on the continent, only to find that tastes, fashions and attitudes are rather different, limiting their scope for profitable expansion. British Airways has attempted to construct a global alliance, including important investments in France and Germany. Despite putting in a great deal of managerial effort and investment, the British Airways shareholders have never seen a profit from Deutsche BA, Air Liberté, or TAT in France. They have encountered considerable regulatory difficulty in growing and developing the businesses in the way that they would like. The British corporate world is littered with the memories and corpses of great British businessmen who thought they could buck the trend and build a successful chain or profitable enterprise on the continent, only to discover that failure stared them in the face.

Technology is going the US way. The latest wave of investment is fuelled by the internet, computers and telecommunications. Everyone agrees that the US is several years ahead of all other parts of the world. All agree that the European continent has been held back by regulation, monopoly and a flight of talent to the more entrepreneurial culture in the US. Businesses looking for the latest technology to enable them to change and adapt would naturally look across the Atlantic rather than across the Channel.

The European continent has also suffered from believing in closed or protected markets. Any British entrepreneur can arrive in Wall Street and, after a few days' or weeks' work, can put together a takeover bid for a US quoted company. Most larger and many medium-sized US companies do have quotes on one or more of the successful US stock markets. Their shares are freely traded, and it is possible for a foreign business to mount a successful takeover bid. Until recently this has been quite impossible on the continent of Europe. Many medium-sized and even larger German and French companies are controlled by shareholders who have no intention of selling out to a foreign bidder. Many German companies are effectively owned by their bankers who wish to keep them as client companies in all senses. Many French and German companies have strong family shareholdings, or crossholdings from other companies in the same or a related industry. Again, these shareholders are usually reluctant to sell out, especially to a foreign bidder. The continent of Europe sees the contested takeover as an undesirable feature of Anglo-Saxon capitalism which it is reluctant to import.

At the beginning of 2000, a British company decided to challenge this orthodoxy in a very dramatic way. Vodaphone Air Touch wanted to buy Mannesmann, the German telecommunications company. It chose its target wisely. Mannesmann was a rare German company with a large number of foreign and independent shareholders open to persuasion if a good takeover bid came along. The German government panicked when it saw the scale and attractiveness of the bid. The Chancellor of Germany himself, Gerhard Schroeder, intervened, condemning the British raiders. Whereas the German government had been very happy to see BMW buy Rover, the British car company, and to see both Rolls-Royce and Bentley passed to German ownership, it felt very differently when there was a proposal that something should go the other way.

The pursuit of the Mannesmann bid was an important development in European markets. It was unlikely to herald a major restructuring of European business. The European bourses are not subject to the same creative and destructive waves of mergers and acquisitions that both the Wall Street and London markets create. There remains deep in continental culture a belief that unless there is general agreement over a takeover bid, it is unsporting to mount one. There still remains a wide nexus of relationships between banks, families, and other shareholders which makes it more difficult for a British or US company to acquire a French or German partner.

It is quite possible for a British or US company to proceed to invest in a greenfield operation, starting from scratch. However, the pace of change worldwide is now so great, and the power of brands so strong, that this is rarely as attractive an option to boards of directors of larger companies as the decision to buy market and market-share, brand and physical equipment through takeover bids. It is also difficult where a licence or other regulatory approval is needed, as continental governments are reluctant to grant permission to new UK competitors.

Post-war US investment

The wave of US investment in Britain began shortly after the war. It was a natural follow-on to the hospitality the US found when it used Britain as the base from which to launch its sea-borne invasion of occupied France and Germany, alongside British allies. The US was deeply involved in the rebuilding of Europe after the disaster of the Second World War. A great deal of US money was pumped into the continent, and US businesses saw the opportunity that US goodwill and cash support would obviously generate. The great names of the

US consumer revolution were alert to the opportunity to base a factory in Britain, both to supply the growing British consumer market as prosperity picked up after 1945, and to use Britain as a base to export onto the continent.

In those early years, the political stability of Britain was an added advantage. The continental countries made investors more nervous. They had, after all, only recently recovered from an extremely damaging war and several of the countries had only just established democratic institutions after a period of tyranny and dictatorship. It took Spain rather longer to emerge from its political troubles than Italy or Germany, where new institutions were set up by the victorious powers after 1945.

There was some comfort to the US investor in the ubiquitous English language: similar standards of accounting, a legal code they could understand – although they no longer shared it – and a general attitude towards the ways of conducting business in an open and honest manner that made sense to US corporate managers. The US brought to Britain its mighty motor industry. Ford made substantial investments to supply the growing British market with popular, sensibly priced cars. General Motors followed later, acquiring Vauxhall, Hillman and other well known British brands. US oil companies increased their presence as motoring took off. Exxon successfully built up the Esso brand in Britain. Mobil, Gulf and others followed suit, alongside homegrown British Petroleum and Anglo-Dutch Shell. Boeing gradually displaced the outclassed British civil airline manufacturing industry as the principal supplier of planes to British-based airlines. This led to important aerospace work for the British aerospace industry, including the successful twinning of Rolls-Royce Engines with Boeing Airframes. The US computer industry arrived in force in the 1970s and 1980s, spawning hi-tech revolution in Silicon Glen in Scotland, near Glasgow; in Silicon Valley along the Thames, and in several other British locations.

In each case the managements felt at home in Britain. They would have their disagreements and they kept some of their US ways, but it was relatively easy going as there was that common cultural understanding. British resentment of US power and success, so obvious during the war and in the immediate post-war period, dulled as British achievements built up and as the US showed its paces worldwide. Why knock its success when the fruits of it could be so enjoyable?

The British and US economies grew closer and closer together in many respects as the Thatcher and Reagan revolutions were unleashed in the 1980s. Both Britain and the US developed mighty worldwide financial service and banking industries. Where Britain had led the world as principal banker and financial service provider in the nineteenth century, based on its success as an imperial and financial power, so the US emerged as a crucial provider of financial services and banking in the latter part of the twentieth century. The remarkable thing was the way in which London managed to increase its lead in some areas and remain an important competitor as well as a trading partner of Wall Street in the latter part of the twentieth century. There are still only three really large stock markets, foreign exchange markets and banking markets in the world. These are New York, London and Tokyo. Everyone agrees that those centres have gained pre-eminence within their respective time zones. There is a flood of global trading which starts as the sun rises in Tokyo, which passes through London and ends up in New York when Tokyo has long since gone to bed.

Both the US and Britain have been in the forefront of pioneering the global services revolution. They have seen that Anglo-Saxon accounting and legal skills can be developed and applied to world markets. They have been in the forefront of creating links around the world so that the same legal or accountancy firm can offer advice based on different national and continental systems on the five continents. Both the US and Britain have benefited from early and thoroughgoing liberalisation of their telecommunication systems. The US began with the decision to allow MCI and Sprint to compete against the Bell Telephone monopoly. Subsequently they decided to split up the Bell Company itself. This was consciously followed in the UK when the Conservative government of the 1980s chose privatisation and liberalisation. When I worked out those policies for the Thatcher government, I based much of them on the remarkable experience of new technology and dynamic growth in the US that had followed from the crucial decisions there.

The result of the different attitude towards services and the ability to project services on a global basis can be seen in the shapes of the different economies. By the late 1990s, manufacturing was down to only 16 per cent of US employment and 18 per cent of the UK's. Conversely, it still remained at 27 per cent in Germany and 23 per cent in Italy. The British and US service sectors were proportionately larger, showing that they had adjusted more rapidly to the global pressures which will shift more and more manufacturing to lower cost parts of the world.

The dominance of Britain and the US in financial service activity is quite startling. In 1998, the UK accounted for 32 per cent of the market in foreign exchange. The US accounted for 18 per cent whereas Germany only accounted for 5 per cent. London's stock market capitalisation is almost double the capitalisation of the Frankfurt and Paris stock markets combined. The UK trades more overseas equity than the US and Japanese markets do together; and they in turn trade much more than the other European stock markets. There are 540 foreign banks with offices in London – more than double the number in Germany, and three times the number in France.

There has been considerable argument in the UK about whether it is right for us to follow the US model to such an extent. Critics of the Americanisation of the British economy claim that the US encourages a much harsher climate for the poor and the unemployed than Germany or France. They claim that the continental system assures people of jobs and security and takes care of them in a much more compassionate way. This is not borne out by the income or unemployment figures. Europe's big problem is the massive increase in unemployment in recent years. The EU outside the UK has found it almost impossible to generate new jobs in the private sector. High levels of taxation and regulation have produced a hostile atmosphere for business. Most of the new jobs and new technologies have come via the US and Asia. Unemployment in France and Germany has in recent years been double the level we now see in the US and the UK. Income levels in the US are considerably higher than in continental countries. It is better to be on a low income in work in the US than out of work and on an even lower benefit income in the EU.

There has also been considerable criticism of the US way of allowing companies to mount takeovers of their competitors and to force change upon reluctant or sleepy managements. Of course, many businessmen would be comforted to think that government interference and regulation guaranteed them a job for life, freeing them from the constraint of having to perform in order to avoid takeover. Unfortunately for the EU, world economic development is not going to be like that. The US model is dominant. US companies have a long reach. US companies account for the ten leading brands in the world and show excellence and drive in a wide range of industrial and service activities. Because the US is the modern colossus, it is inevitable that much of the US style will work its way round the world.

The different responses of Britain, on the one hand, and France and Germany, on the other, are instructive. Since the 1980s, when the UK has tried to copy more of the US model with lower taxes, lower government spending and less regulation than adopted on the continent, the British economy has performed much better and has caught up with the US to a greater extent than France and Germany. Britain is now the fourth largest economy in the world after only the US, Japan and Germany. After adjusting for the larger number of people in Germany, Britain is better off per head than Germany, and better off than most of the other EU countries. This has been achieved through huge changes in the UK economy. In the motor industry we have seen the decline and fall of all indigenous motor manufacturing. There are only a handful of companies left producing specialist vehicles in small numbers that are British-owned and British-managed. The UK has welcomed the wave of investment and management from the United States and from Japan, more recently from France and Germany, to transform its car industry and rebuild it. BMW has found the task of owning and managing Rover too difficult, but Peugeot has been more successful making cars in the UK. A weak Euro in 2000 put considerable pressure on many manufacturing businesses in the UK where they compete against continental rivals.

The City revolution was triggered by the UK government decision to open the City up to much more foreign capital and competition. The City went through a rapid metamorphosis at the end of the 1980s which fuelled the phenomenal growth of the 1990s as the City stretched its lead over other European financial centres. In telecommunications, the UK went from being one of the laggards amongst the developed world into one of the world leaders. Britain has been at the forefront of developing mobile telephony and digital communication.

Exchange rates and economic performance

We can see the same convergence of the US and British economies in the performance of our currencies. At the end of the 1980s and in the early 1990s, the UK decided to hitch its fortunes more strongly to those on the continent. Before joining the Exchange Rate Mechanism (ERM) Britain tried to keep sterling in line with the Deutschmark. It led to interest rates too low for the UK and a substantial monetary expansion. For a while it created good times. There is always a delay before inflation takes off. We then entered the mechanism and had to keep sterling stable at DM2.95 until the markets forced us out in September 1992. The price of keeping our currency in line with the Deutschmark was colossal. In the late 1980s, when sterling had wanted to go up, it was held down only at the price of a monetary explosion. The government printed money to sell sterling on the market to try to keep it down. Interest rates were kept low to deter foreign deposits in the UK. In the early 1990s inflation picked up as a result. Then the process reversed. Sterling wanted to go down. Interest rates were sent sky-high and money policy tightened dramatically. Recession naturally followed.

If we take the performance of sterling from the beginning of 1993 when the impact of being in the ERM had worn off, and sterling could settle down to a new lower level against the Deutschmark, we can see that sterling has for a period of seven years been extremely stable against the dollar. Between 1993 and 2000, sterling never fell by more than 6 per cent from its then dollar level, and never rose by more than 12 per cent from its then rate. Conversely, sterling has been much less stable against the Deutschmark, rising from DM2.20 to DM3.40. During our time in the ERM, sterling was very unstable against the dollar, damaging our business with the US. US tourists were priced out of London. All those dealing in dollar commodities and products were put under considerable pressure.

The relative stability of the dollar/pound exchange rate can be accounted for by the strong two-way pulls across the Atlantic. With the US as the biggest overseas investor in the UK, and the UK in turn the biggest overseas investor in the US, it means that there are strong flows of investment monies, dividends and interest payments going both ways. The City of London transacts most of its business in dollars, and as one of the world's premier financial centres, alongside New York and Tokyo, the huge volume of London-based transactions is another important factor. Most of the UK's hi-tech exports – such as aerospace, wholesale pharmaceuticals, software, computers and microchips – are priced in dollars. The main commodity markets, including the metals, oil, gas and soft commodities, trade in dollars.

The US is the UK's biggest single export market, accounting for more than Germany and France combined when taking visibles and invisibles together.

Many in manufacturing want a stable pound/dollar rate, and since we left the ERM, we have largely enjoyed one. People do not always get what they want in business life. There was no particular reason why the pound should be stable against the dollar. The government wasn't trying to engineer such a controlled exchange rate. No government could marshal enough money to intervene to hold the exchange rate for any length of time, given the enormous flows going across the exchanges between sterling and dollars. The stability shows that over this quite extended time period there have been enough similarities in the trading pattern of the US and British economies and in the conduct of their respective monetary policies for the two rates to stay more or less in line. The authorities are forced into very similar responses when conducting their interest rate financial policies because the two economies are subject to very similar pressures and they are at a similar stage in the economic cycle. We have resumed turbulence against the Deutschmark and Euro as a result. There are signs in 2000 that the authorities want to lower the pound against the dollar, and some signs that as the UK adopts more EU characteristics it loses ground against the US currency.

The dominance of Anglo-Saxon capitalism is now everywhere to be seen. Whilst the US is clearly the senior partner, the UK has been no slouch in building global business and coat-tailing behind the US. A study for *Business Week* in July 1999 of the world's most valuable companies underlined this success. Whilst the US could account for 494 of the top 1000 companies in the world by value of their shares, Britain was in second place with 108 companies worth $2 trillion, just ahead of Japan's 120 slightly smaller companies, worth $1.9 trillion. Germany, with 36 companies worth $820 billion; France, with 45 companies worth $756 billion; and Italy, with 23 companies worth $380 billion, were between them smaller than Britain when measuring the global reach and market power of their companies. Indeed, it was interesting to see that Switzerland was ahead of Italy, proving that from a small mountain base not part of the EU itself, Switzerland was able to provide a good home for multinational companies operating in the five continents of the world, an exercise in considerable market power.

The other interesting thing about the *Business Week* table was that Britain, out of all the countries on the list, achieved the highest returns on capital. Some of the techniques of Anglo-Saxon and now global capitalism have been pioneered first in Britain. Whilst in the 1960s and 1970s it was common for British people to apply American management styles and manuals to their businesses, in the 1980s and 1990s the United Kingdom added something of its own, which enabled it to some extent to return the management fire across the Atlantic. BP's acquisition of Sohio brought home to the US corporate world that British capitalism also had some claws.

The language of business

More important, perhaps, than the facts and figures of the great Anglo-Saxon markets and the global reach of their companies is the feeling in Britain that we are getting closer to the US than to the continent. The common language is a very important force which is drawing us closer together just as Churchill had forecast. Whilst Churchill honestly admitted that he could not foretell the final form the union of the English-speaking peoples would take, he would feel vindicated seeing how English is now the driving force behind many of the new connections and much of the new technology. English is the language of the internet. It is the language of computer software and intelligent systems. It is the language of business consultants, corporate advisers, management advisers and international managements worldwide.

English is also the cultural language of the dominant group on the planet. British television serves up a regular diet of US sitcoms, westerns, US movies. The Hollywood influence is everywhere and frequent, on widescreen and narrow screen. British people welcome Hollywood stars into their living rooms, on television, in tabloid newspapers, and on the radio, as if they were long-lost friends. The fact that they talk the same language makes it easier to accept them as everyday parts of individuals' lives. The tabloid newspaper editor is always screaming to the staff to bring more stories on stars and royals. The Royal Family lives in that star-studded kingdom that mixes Hollywood with big business, with the top of government. Beneath the Star Spangled Banner there is a new global jet-set of stars and their allies. Others have stars in their eyes.

US cultural imperialism began as a good business proposition. The early successes of the US lay more in exporting the hardware of the US way of life. It has more recently evolved to export the ideas and the English language that go with it. The global giants in the inter-war period were the large US motor manufacturers, the oil companies, and the producers of exciting new products like Coca-Cola and Pepsi. The US brought to the world the hamburger, the drive-in, the movie, fast food and the supermarket in the post-war world. All of these things have become a regular part of British daily life. They slid effortlessly across the Atlantic and are no longer seen as raw imports or something exotic and foreign.

Cola and hamburgers: Britain in the diner

If people consciously choose to go out to an Italian or French restaurant, they have a sense of some ethnic differences in cuisine, strengthened by the different language spoken if the restaurant is authentic. Choosing to go to an Italian or French restaurant is rather like choosing to go to a Chinese or a Japanese restaurant. You go because you like the culture, you like its differences, and you expect it to feel foreign. You are consciously adventuring, trying something different. Conversely, when we go to McDonald's or to a Kentucky Fried Chicken outlet there is no similar sense of ethnic adventure. Many people would do so without realising it was a US import. The staff are self-consciously normal British kids with the mongrel mixture of accents you would expect depending on where in the country the restaurant is based. There is less shock and less sense of novelty than going to a restaurant themed to one of our continental partners.

Britain goes to Hollywood

The same is even truer of films, books and plays. Again, the language barrier is the prime difference. If you wish to go to see a good French or Italian film, you will be wrestling with subtitles or your own grasp – or lack of it – of the language. A US film will have different accents, but usually as the film develops people suspend their disbelief and regard it as part of their cultural inheritance as well. The US and the UK share a language and a literature. Americans regard Shakespeare as their dramatist and often make pilgrimages to Stratford to celebrate his success. British citizens are familiar with Huckleberry Finn, Tom Sawyer, westerns and Henry James. Whilst the British tradition is more maritime and the US more new frontier, both are literatures of adventure, of venturing against the odds, of battling with the mighty sea, or fighting with the Indians for control of the mighty plains. English boys will re-enact the cowboy struggles against the Indians as if it were their heritage. They are not so keen to be Napoleon or the Kaiser in war games.

The new wave of technology puts the US in the driving seat. As I sit writing my book on a modern word processor, I am regularly told I have misspelt a word because I have followed the English rather than the US spelling. The computer games and databanks are in US English. We accept them. Most of us do not rant and rave against US success. We do not have the problem the French have of fighting to keep their language and culture going in a world which is anglicising rapidly.

There are British people who resent US success and would rather join a polyglot European culture, but they are in a minority. I find that those who are most fanatical about us joining a European political union usually betray with their own choice of words a feeling of otherness from the continent. They ask me how often I go to Europe, and are surprised when I say I am nearly always in Europe, for Europe is my continent. Many in Britain still talk about whether we join Europe, failing to see that geographically we are a series of offshore European islands, and that politically we joined part of the European scheme a long time ago. We are now a polyglot people living a varied cultural life. We watch US movies, are becoming more dependent on our cars, may soon be regularly driving to the gym to use the walking machines, and are happy to see the mushrooming of US corporations on the high street and in the industrial parks.

Drinking the odd cappuccino, liking continental as well as New World wines, going to Spain on holiday and admiring some older European cities, is a European attachment, but it is only part of our story. The English language, the ubiquitous cola and hamburgers, and the all-conquering might of US capital makes us mid-Atlantic. Most British people do not want to become Americans, but you are more likely to see them praising Hollywood than French culture, and more likely to see them sipping a rum and cola than downing a grappa. The Atlantic is 3000 miles narrow, and the Channel is 30 miles wide, thanks to the difference of language and customs.

6
The United States of America and the United States of Europe

The coming conflicts

The United States of Europe is being fashioned from a strong anti-Americanism. The United States of America needs to prepare for the coming conflicts. Many great nations have been created or resurrected on the back of a defined antipathy. The US itself began by a passionate revolt against colonial government from the UK. France and Britain have often defined themselves by competing against each other for territory and glory or fighting over styles of government. China and Japan dislike each other intensely, as only close neighbours can.

The danger of emerging European nationalism is that it will be born in this crude image. Many of the fathers and progenitors of the United States of Europe think its role is to challenge the world's current dominant superpower, the US.

There is an important distinction between aggressive nationalism and sensible cultural patriotism. I am very patriotic about my country. It means I am at ease with its history, its culture, its past and its future. It means that I do not wish to see my country run down. I support our teams in sporting competitions. I have a penchant for the music, the landscape, the literature and the traditions of my country. It does not mean that at the same time I have to run down the culture, language and legitimate ambitions of other countries. It means I believe Britain and other countries have a place in the world without conflict. We can enjoy each other's differences whilst resting secure in the knowledge that ours is right for us.

Narrow nationalists transmute their love for country into a hatred of others. They set ambitions for their country that involve treading on the toes of other nations. They do not know where to stop when supporting national teams. Aggressive nationalism can be allied to racism, to a sense of supremacy and right. It leads to verbal abuse and physical violence against others from different races or nations.

The danger, in the creation of a United States of Europe (USE), rests in this fundamental paradox. I am quite sure that those who wish to create a United States of Europe hate narrow nationalism and racism at the level of the individual European country. They rightly perceive that nationalism, racism and fanaticism under the German Reich wrought great atrocities and barbarisms in the 1930s and 1940s. They rightly wish to put behind them an era when France competed for territory against Germany and the other Latin countries, when Spain set out on conquest, and a period when Germany wished to spread her borders east and west by violent means. They loathe Nazism and all its works and are understandably alarmed by the rise of new neo-Nazi groups on the continent. I entirely agree with them that an end to narrow, racial, aggressive competitive nationalism in Western Europe is good.

The irony is that they are in danger of replacing the petty nationalisms of the nations of Europe with an aggressive nationalism of their own at the European level. It is born of a sense of superiority of the European system to any other. It is based on the assumption that Europe needs to challenge the US for supremacy, it needs to get even with the US, and in some fields needs to surpass it. It is competitive and aggressive, but not yet racist or violent.

The idea of a United States of Europe, which looks so appealing to some French and German politicians, can look very threatening from other parts of the world. The common borders that Europe seeks are only common frontiers within part of the EU area. They will be allied to a restrictive immigration policy against all those seeking a better life from the Arab, African and Asian lands beyond. To struggling farmers in the third world, the sound of the gates clanking shut around Fortress Europe is not an attractive sound. To the makers of industrial products from outside Europe who find themselves confronted with a range of non-tariff barriers to trade, the growing central power in Brussels is far from good. The country which should worry most about the emergence of a baby super-state in Europe is the US itself. The USE may as yet have few offensive intercontinental weapons and no military intention against the USA, but it is growing rapidly in power and pretension.

The United States of Europe will have command of united armies of more than 2 million people in arms, and a substantial navy and air force. However, these forces will not have the technological expertise and intercontinental capability of the US forces, and there is no immediate sign that the continental governments are prepared to tax their people more to spend at anything like the level of US defence spending. There is every sign that European forces will remain strongest at home, without the ability to deploy rapidly on a big scale in other parts of the world.

There is, however, clear indication that the European governments first wish to confront the US economically. One of the most cited reasons for creating a new currency, the Euro, is that Europeans want to have a currency that rivals the US dollar. It is difficult to understand why this would be in the interests of the Western European peoples unless it is the intention to create an economic area and then a state which can rival the US.

The Euro

In 1999, eleven countries agreed to go ahead and replace their own currencies with the Euro. France, Germany, Belgium, Holland, Austria, Finland and Luxembourg were always expected to be in. They were joined as founder members by Portugal, Spain, Ireland and Italy. These countries had more difficulty in meeting the requirements, but as the leading members had also found the criteria awkward, every country bar Greece, who wanted to join, was allowed in. This left four members of the EU outside the first grouping of Euroland. The UK and Denmark had opt-outs from the scheme and decided for the time being to say 'No'. Greece was not allowed in because its economy was so out of line with the rest. Subsequently, its main economic figures improved and it will be allowed to join at the same time as the others. Sweden decided against immediate entry, even though under the Treaty it was meant to join with the others.

The participating currencies locked exchange rates against the Euro. People and businesses can now carry out transactions in each country either in its own currency or in Euros, with the exchange taking place at the agreed rate. In 2002, notes and coin in Euros will be issued generally for the first time, and the old currencies of the member countries will be phased out over a six-month period. Since its launch as a trading currency on 1 January 1999 the new currency has fallen sharply against the dollar, yen and sterling.

At its launch at the beginning of 1999 extravagant claims were made for the Euro. Many around the world took them quite seriously. European bankers and politicians claimed that the Euro would soon build up to be of similar importance in world trade to the mighty dollar, and then in due course might surpass it. They painted a picture of millions of traders around the world having to buy Euros to trade in, taking pleasure in helping build a rival to the US dollar. Things have not worked out quite as they envisaged, but it still remains their aim. They will be more successful in building a bigger transaction volume in Euros when they force people to adopt the Euro in 2002. French and German, Italian and Spanish people have been very reluctant to adopt the Euro voluntarily, but when the notes and coin are introduced they will have no choice, as the old currencies will cease to be legal tender.

Ireland has found early membership of the Euro area difficult. Irish interest rates had to be lowered sharply to get down to the general Euro rate. The big increase in credit which followed has pushed up Irish inflation, leaving the country short of means to tackle this problem.

Airbus

EU governments seem to believe that if they can build a substantial currency which third parties wish to trade in, invest in, and hold in their bank accounts, they will have made their first important dent in the economic power of the US and the dollar. They are promoting many other forms of rivalry. The most intense has taken place in the field of civil aircraft manufacture. The huge costs of researching and developing new planes had led, ineluctably, to monopoly or cartel in the world market, dominated by a few large US corporations, and especially by Boeing. The EU decided that it, too, must create a big centre of civil aircraft manufacture to rival that of the US. In one sense this was public spirited from the world's point of view. There is no doubt that competition and choice is a good thing and the arrival of the Airbus has empowered airlines to compare deals across the Atlantic to create some pressure for lower prices. If this had been the only reason for the European adventure, I would have been happy to praise their benign nature.

Unfortunately, it is quite clear from reading their words and listening to their statements that the creators of Airbus had in mind a very traditional and old-fashioned type of commercial rivalry. They decided that whatever the cost in terms of public subsidy, government orders and encouragement, Europe would have its own civil aviation industry. In the big bidding competitions between Boeing and Airbus to win the business, some of the freer spirits in the European aviation world portrayed the battle as a titanic struggle between the good and the bad, the European and the US. The process of bitter commercial contest soon spilled over into government against government, lobbying and dispute.

The Americans claimed that in the early days Airbus attracted massive subsidy and in later days attracted easy-terms finance in the form of launch aid which would not have been available from the marketplace. They regarded this as unfair. The Europeans countered with their argument that Boeing received hidden subsidies, being generously rewarded for its defence contracts which the company had used to cross-subsidise civil aircraft manufacture. There may be some truth in both sets of allegations. The deliberate creation of a rival business to a large US combine which has close relationships with the US government has led directly to a festering trade dispute. The world airline passenger may be better off, and the airlines undoubtedly have more choice as a result, but Euro–US relations have taken a move for the worse as a result of this European attempt to pitch against US dominance in a given area.

Agriculture

In the two big areas where the EU already has almost complete control over the policies of the nations of Western Europe, agriculture and trade, a number of disputes have blown up between the EU and the US. In the agricultural field, the EU has banned imports of US beef on the grounds that the US farmers use hormones to improve the quality and to make their farming more efficient. The EU claims that these hormones could be damaging to health, yet they have failed to produce any evidence to sustain this contention. The US could point to the fact that it has had no rash of illnesses or premature deaths amongst its people based on their beef-eating habits.

The EU can counter by saying that many people in the EU do not like the idea of hormone-based beef and that the European government is merely speaking for them. A fairer way of tackling the problem would be clear labelling, leaving the customers of Europe the same choice as the customers in the US as to whether they wished to buy hormone-based beef or not. If the hormone-based beef is a better quality for a given price, as the Americans claim, some will wish to purchase it in the marketplace. Others of a purer frame of mind might wish to buy organically reared beef at a higher price.

The obstinate refusal of the EU to allow customer choice in this field has naturally alienated US opinion. The US claims that it has many more efficient farmers and that it is being penalised in order to support less efficient European producers in their domestic market. The US has also been able to retaliate by pointing out that some of the beef reared in the EU has been reared in herds contaminated by BSE, which the EU itself has decided is extremely dangerous. The irony has not been lost on US commentators.

Trade wars

The beef war has been mirrored in several other areas of trade. A regular spectre at the feast is that of the banana wars. Several EU countries were imperial powers. Since shedding colonial responsibility they have nonetheless retained an affection and special links with a number of third world banana producers who like to sell their product into the European market. The UK, for example, has close links with the Windward and Leeward Islands, and Jamaica, who have traditionally supplied many of the bananas into the UK market.

The banana producers closest to the EU have enjoyed favoured arrangements to the exclusion of so-called dollar bananas coming from parts of Latin America where US influence is stronger. The US claims that the dollar bananas are bigger, better and cheaper than those produced in the Caribbean and sold on special terms into the EU. The US took its case to the World Trade Organization, which found in favour of the US, and told the EU to remove the favoured protective arrangements that were in place. The EU has so far failed to comply with this requirement, and the US is angrily trying to get satisfaction through international legal means. It has also led to US retaliation. The US has announced categories of imports from the EU which will attract high tariffs as a warning against what the US sees as unfair trading.

More recently, we have fallen into rum wars. Bacardi of Bermuda, and France's Pernod Ricard both seek the rights to the Havana Club trademark, a coveted brand in the rum world. The Havana Club rum factory was confiscated by Fidel Castro. France's Pernod Ricard acquired the rights from the Cuban business. Meanwhile, the US says that the rights belong to Bacardi, which bought the rights from the Cuban plant's original owners who owned them before the expropriation by Fidel Castro.

Once again there are rights on both sides, but the EU has failed to understand the true causes of US anger and the dispute is gaining a nasty political edge. To the US trade negotiators, the de facto recognition of Fidel Castro's expropriation of assets inherent in the French claim is unacceptable. The US has had a very fraught relationship with Cuba, not least during the period of the extremely dangerous Cuban missile crisis, and cannot easily forgive the expropriations by its arch-communist antagonist so close to its borders. The Europeans believe that Castro is the de facto leader of Cuba, and that he has established control over the assets expropriated from former owners. They believe the French company has acquired them in a legal and sensible manner and their claim ought to be upheld.

When it comes to international negotiations over freer trade, it is all too often the case that the US and Europe find themselves on different sides. US trade policy was directed by Charlene Barshefsky for President Clinton. Europe's is directed by the French socialist Pascal Lamy. These two were unlikely to agree. Lamy's socialism was one obstacle, and his belief that the world must be kept free from US domination was another. The socialist mindset of the European trade position is favourable to European protectionism. They see nothing wrong with subsidies, restraints on trade, tariff barriers and the like, as legitimate weapons in the war for economic supremacy around the world.

Both the US and Europe run protected and subsidised agricultural systems. Both engage in a macabre dance in world trade talks over whether any of this elaborate structure can be removed without an unreasonable political backlash in the farming heartlands of the US

Midwest, or amongst the small and not very profitable farms of Germany and France in Europe. Despite this convergence of view on some agricultural matters, nearly everything sparks problems in the world trading system, producing a divergence of opinion between the US and the united Europe.

The question we need to answer is, 'How serious could this set of tensions and conflicts become?' The pattern so far is that as Europe gains control over an area, so it produces policies and attitudes of mind that are hostile to the US. There is no sign of resolution of beef hormones, bananas or rum. There is every sign that the number of items on the list in the trade disputes will lengthen as time goes on. Similarly, as the European currency eventually takes off, when it becomes mandatory in the eleven Euroland countries, it is highly likely that the rhetoric of confrontation will be intensified and the Europeans will start claiming early victories in the battle of the giants. Each of these economic and financial disputes then comes to take on a wider significance and gain a more worrying political edge.

Europe goes it alone on foreign policy

Until recently, the US has not taken any of this very seriously. They have decided that dialling one number for Europe has all sorts of advantages and believe that the trade rows are just teething problems as the new European state attempts to position itself. Now that Europe is talking about creating a defence identity – in other words, having its own army, navy and air force – and a common foreign policy, the US policy establishment in Washington is having second thoughts. There is absolutely no reason to suppose that European foreign policy as it develops will be compatible with, or even friendly towards US foreign policy. The self-same people who have decided that the Euro should topple the dollar, that Airbus should overwhelm Boeing, and that European farming methods will exclude the Midwest, are now out to design a foreign policy and a defence policy for their fledgeling European state. US policy-makers are at last realising that this foreign policy will be designed by people who are deeply distrustful of the US and would dearly love to see it removed from its position of world supremacy.

There have been two warning signs that have shaken US policy-makers so far. The first occurred shortly after German reunification. The US was an enthusiastic proponent of the greater Germany and thought that the greater Germany might lead on to the greater Europe. President Bush's administration, keen to foster it, was dismayed when Germany immediately opened negotiations with the Soviet Union and developed a special relationship with the emerging Russia. The US is still very worried about the stability and long-term intentions of Russia, and is not very keen on Germany's *Ostpolitik* extending to Moscow.

The second worry emerged when Germany recognised Croatia in 1995, dragging the rest of the EU into similar action at a time when the US judged that recognition of Croatia would intensify the simmering civil war in the Balkans. The EU's action was followed up by a lack of resolve and a lack of troops to sort out the problem. It ended in embarrassment with the Europeans unable to handle a crisis in their own backyard. The US flirted with the policy of allowing the Europeans to solve the crisis on their own, only to discover that European diplomacy was pointing in the wrong direction on many occasions, and was allied to a weakness in military resolve that proved fatal. The crisis took much longer and involved much more loss of life and many more complexities than the US would have liked. Many in the US policy establishment blame EU diplomatic and military leadership for the blunders which followed.

The emerging attitudes in Western Europe could lead to some strengthening of isolationism in the US. If the EU decides to provoke the US in an ever-wider range of areas, many more in the US will say, 'let them stew in their own juice'. The main thing which holds back the serious US policy establishment from saying this is the potential threat of Russia if it fell into the wrong hands, and the need for the US to have a first line of defence somewhere on the European continent. The British allies of the US have always understood this need. The UK helped the US with the installation of Cruise missiles as a line of defence on European soil at a time when some other countries in Western Europe were unhelpful or downright hostile to the endeavour. The same role may be needed on the part of friendly European countries in the latest US development of a missile shield and early warning system.

If all goes according to the plans of the progenitors of the European state, anti-American feeling will build up gradually and will spread to a whole range of policy areas. Europeans will be taught that US foodstuff is not fit to eat, that US planes are not as good as European ones, that the US is the evil force in the environmental world, doing more damage than any other country to the planet, that European foreign policy has to put European interests first and may not extend to being part of a US pan-Western defence system. Both France and Germany are much friendlier to Russia than the US has been in the last 50 years, and both would probably like to see an end to US troops in Europe. There is little doubt that a European government in Brussels will be anti-American, and will regard it as a sign of success if the relationship between the two deteriorates at a suitable pace.

This will be a tragedy in the making. It is not in the interests of either Europe or the US to allow more tensions to develop and the relationship to become strained. The US does have an interest in the defence of democracy and freedom around the world. The US does need some defence collaboration on the continent of Europe for its own interests, as well as for European interests. The EU for its part will have to accept that it is not prepared to put the effort, money and technology into a sufficient defence for Western Europe and is dependent upon the US alliance. The EU should understand that, given US technological superiority in so many fields, collaboration and friendly competition in the private sector is a much better route than head-to-head government confrontation and an attempt to close markets against each other's goods and services. It is important for people on both sides to understand the deep resentments that underlie the European strategy and for the US to turn to those allies within the EU and parts of the European continent that are friendly and understand the need for a good relationship.

The next steps in the conflict

The next steps in the conflict are also all too easy to forecast. Trade disputes will intensify as more and more items are found on both sides that irritate and annoy. We can expect to see a series of EU decisions designed to favour domestic European businesses at the expense of US ones in fields as wide-ranging as media, telephony, internet technology and transport. In the aviation field, those who wish to construct alliances amongst dominant European carriers normally find the going in Brussels easy, whereas those who wish to include a major US company in their alliance find it much more difficult. In media, there will be an attempt in the name of defending

French and German culture to resist the growing global claims of the large US corporations. In the world of internet and telephony, there will be attempts to impose European standards that are not necessarily compatible with US ones and a battle over who has the right to settle these kind of issues. There will be many more agricultural disputes, and further rows over trading relationships with former colonies and countries in respective spheres of influence.

More worrying will be the widening of the foreign policy disputes to cover ever more areas. It will not consist solely of disputes about the Balkans that result from the growing confidence of the EU in a united European foreign policy. There will be different attitudes towards the Middle East, towards the Arab world, and towards Asia. European defence evolution in itself is going to cause tensions within NATO and will alarm some Americans. The more independent the EU becomes, the less inclined the US will be to share technology, intelligence and information with its former European allies. We have already had a taster of this with the EU objecting to British involvement in intelligence-gathering with the Americans in a combined defence operation. The EU is now claiming that this has extended into the field of commercial espionage and shows that Britain is on the wrong side in the trade war.

Ideological adversaries

The EU adventure is hostile to many Anglo-Saxon values. The leading English-speaking countries believe in free trade, democracy, free speech, liberty, freedom of association, religious tolerance, competition, enterprise and choice. The EU for its part has rather different values. It believes in solidarity, cooperation, partnership, corporate solutions, European champions, some limitations upon the freedom of speech and the support of good order and consensus values above liberty. There will undoubtedly be a clash as the years pass between the corporatist, bureaucratic virtues of the EU and the liberty-seeking outspokenness of the Anglo-Saxon countries. The EU is careless about democracy, usually preferring secretive bureaucracy.

The differences are very clear in the attitude towards democracy itself. The EU has decided to create a government before creating a strong parliament or congress. In the UK, a strong Parliament emerged to impose limitations on the power of the Crown, and more recently, upon the power of the elected executive government. In the

US, the Congress was formed to defend people's liberties, to give voice to their worries and grievances, and to provide strong scrutiny over the actions of the president, who was in turn directly elected.

The European Parliament is almost an afterthought, a presentational device rather than a serious spanner in the works of executive government. The European Parliament has no power to tax, whereas the British Parliament and the US Senate and House of Representatives are based upon the power to grant or withhold tax revenues to the government. The European Parliament has very little influence over legislation and has no direct entitlement to legislate. Conversely, both the British Parliament and the US representative houses can initiate legislation, and are solely responsible for deciding its fate.

The executive government of the EU, formed out of the Commission, is made up of unelected people. In Britain, most Ministers of the Crown are elected, and all have to be in one of the two chambers of Parliament subject to scrutiny. In the US, most senior office-holders go through an election before they gain their position, including judges as well as governors, and of course the president himself. In the EU, the most powerful people in the government, the Commissioners, are selected by member state governments and are not directly answerable to the European Parliament. They are never Members of the European Parliament, and when they go there they are not nearly as accountable as British Ministers in the House of Commons. People on the continent just do not believe that such strong scrutiny of the executive is a necessary or desirable part of good government. They have come to accept that government is often a matter of self-serving bureaucracies, that much of it is conducted behind closed doors, and that elections settle very little. Italy has become used to seeing administrations come and go, as the proportional representation system used in Italy rarely delivers a decisive result at a general election. In Germany, the government has only changed once in the post-war period, as a result of votes cast in a general election when Chancellor Kohl was thrown out of office. On other occasions the government has changed as a result of decisions by politicians behind closed doors changing their allegiances and shifting coalitions.

In the US, one or other of the main parties wins the presidency, and has a four-year period to change the shape and direction of the country (and the president can only hold office for two consecutive terms). In the UK, majority governments are usually produced by the electors and held to account by the electors at a subsequent general election. This creates a very different relationship between the electors and the elected than in a proportional representation system where the important decisions are taken after the election, when the deal-making and coalition-building begins. On the continent, many ministers are not elected, heads of state and government are not subject to the same degree of press, parliamentary and congressional scrutiny, and political elites contain debate within narrow confines.

Could the EU be democratic?

Some European partners had hoped that the British involvement in the EU in general, and in the European Parliament in particular, would give more democratic incisiveness and legitimacy to the European government. They have been disappointed as, for a variety of reasons, successive British governments have been unwilling to see big powers passed to the European Parliament, whilst the Commission and the bureaucracy of Brussels have fought a usually successful action to make sure that they are not directly accountable to the European Parliament in the same way as a British Minister is to the UK Parliament. If Anglo Saxons were designing a new country called the United States of Europe, they would begin by trying to gain consent to the proposition through a public campaign followed by a general election to a much more powerful European Parliament. Out of that Parliament ministers would be chosen. Political debate would soon be organised in trans-European parties representing the different points of view on European issues, and ministers would be brought regularly to account before that Parliament. Alternatively, following the US model, the president of the European Commission would be directly elected by all the peoples of the member countries of the Union, and he or she in turn would be directly answerable to the media day to day and to the electorate at the presidential election. Europe has eschewed either model, reluctant to see so much prying into the affairs of the European government. This has created more mistrust in the Anglo-Saxon world than if a more democratic system had been adopted.

There are similar disagreements between the English-speaking approach and that of the continent when it comes to free speech.

British and US democracy is based on the proposition that people should be free to say what they wish, to associate with whom they wish, to run for office and to form parties to make a lively democratic debate. Neither Britain nor the US has been troubled in the last century by either a strong fascist or a strong communist movement. There was a murky period in US history when suspected communists were purged from office, but most Americans now look on that era with a distaste that reflects their underlying belief in the right of individuals to express opinions and to fight for them in a democratic way.

In contrast, the continent has been grossly disfigured by both communist and fascist activities over much of the last 100 years. The impact of Nazism and fascism in Italy and Spain on the political process has been very marked. Indeed, it would be surprising if it were not. It has meant that many in the governing elites in those countries are suspicious of giving people the right to free speech, fearing that baser instincts might prevail and extreme parties and attitudes re-emerge. The EU is adopting a high and mighty tone, seeking ways to determine whether parties are suitable to run for office or not, and seeking to outlaw certain political attitudes and choice of phrases from the political debate altogether.

The Anglo-Saxon approach says that there should be a law of libel and a law to prevent racism and other undesirable traits. Under such a law a politician is governed by the same criminal law as the rest of the community. As long as he or she does not go over the criminal boundary in what he or she wishes to do or say, that person is then free to express his or her views and to debate them openly. The EU is not prepared to rely on the long shot of criminal action against those who are clearly beyond the pale, but is seeking to narrow the wide range of political views on the continent by those in power actually determining what is and is not a reasonable attitude for the political debate. Anglo Saxons find this all rather scary, as it gives undue power to those who are already in government to control the access to power of those who would challenge them.

Free trade

The English-speaking world strongly believes in freer trade. It is true that there have been imperfections in both the US and British approach to free trade, especially in the agricultural areas, but, as we will see in the next chapter, the general thrust of trade policy on both sides of the Atlantic, in the UK and the US, is towards the reduction or abolition of tariffs, the reduction or abolition of subsidies and state intervention, and the development of a healthy and competitive market. On the continent of Europe, attitudes are rather different. French policy in particular is driven by a wish to create French national champion companies. This is now being supplanted in the minds of both the French and Brussels by the wish to create Euro-champions capable of taking on the mighty US and Japanese corporations. There is not the same wish on the continent to create conditions in which small companies, entrepreneurs, and foreign competitors can challenge the existence of the mighty established corporations. In the US, whenever a large corporation becomes so successful that it has a dominant position in the marketplace, the politicians and government usually intervene to break it up. They successfully broke up the giant Rockefeller oil company earlier in the twentieth century, the Bell telephone company in the 1980s, and are now taking similar action against Microsoft at the beginning of the twenty-first century. If the Franco-German alliance had such a giant company, with such a strong position in world markets, they would be inclined to back it and help it, rather than break it up in the US way.

Continental economies have found it very difficult to create conditions in which entrepreneurs thrive, small businesses set up and a lively competitive challenge to existing corporations emerges. In contrast, the US has been very good at this. In recent years the UK has moved nearer to the US than to the continental European experience. It comes down to the difference in cultures. The EU believes in a cosy relationship between government and the large corporations. The Anglo-Saxon world believes in a more sceptical and distant relationship where government intervenes only when it feels the corporations have gone too far, in order to protect the market or to restore competition.

Anglo Saxons are very worried about any suggestion that government is corrupt, self-serving, or has too cosy a relationship with those who are being governed. European government is much happier with the idea of ease of access and frequent transition between the different members of the governing elites in business, academic life and government. The UK has been strongest in seeking to expose the graft, corruption and incompetence in much EU budgeting. Each year, the Court of Auditors produces a long list of mistakes and irregularities in the handling of large EU funds. Each year the Commission promises to do better and then regularly buries the report and fails to follow it up. The EU's attitude towards corruption is so lax that when a middle-ranking official, Paul van Buitenen, decided to blow the whistle on a big scandal, the EU retaliated by suspending him from his job rather than by taking action to tackle the underlying problem he had revealed. In the US and in the UK, politicians are much more hostile to the idea of corruption and incompetence. Senatorial inquiries, Select Committee inquiries in Britain, strong parliamentary debate, and an intrusive media on both sides of the Atlantic are regularly able to expose corruption, waste and incompetence as a means of encouraging all those in government to follow a straighter and narrower path than in the EU.

We can see a similar difference in attitudes in the approach to green issues. On both sides of the Atlantic in the Anglo-Saxon world, people want to look after the environment and value the forest and field, valley and mountain. They also believe, however, that a prosperous country needs to keep its people warm and needs to be mobile. People do not see motorists or users of central heating systems as criminals who should be banned or controlled. Conversely, on the continent, there is a much more entrenched green lobby. Proportional representation systems mean they often get people elected to their respective parliaments. There is a consensus view on the continent that all environmental protection measures are good and necessary, whatever impact they may have on the prosperity machine of business. It goes with the general view that the consensus should be sought, the politically fashionable should always be given strong support, and that dissenting views are undesirable.

In the Anglo-Saxon world, the man or woman with a different idea, with a better way of doing things, with the enterprising company, with the challenging theory, with the uncomfortable propensity to caricature or to criticise the powers that be, the satirist, the cartoonist, the witty columnist, are all revered and valued. Independence of mind and spirit is at a premium. This leads naturally to commercial success, to an outward-going approach, to trading in the five continents and oceans of the world, and to a belief in the diversity of political life and political debate. On the continent, there is a rather different view. People value belonging to elites, seeking consensus, confining disagreements behind closed doors, finding ways of smoothing the passage of large corporations, forging partnerships, confining disagreeable or outspoken debate and regarding those who challenge or think differently as a threat rather than a stimulus to a more prosperous future. This big cultural and attitudinal difference between the EU on the continent, and the Anglo-Saxon world, lies behind many of the disputes that it is now our task to chronicle. US policy, which for several years has felt it was a good idea to unite Europe, is coming to see that unification could be a mistake for US influence in the world, and for continuing good relations with the individual nations that now make up the EU.

The development of tensions between the EU and the US will happen gradually over an ever-widening range of areas. We will see how disagreements in trade policy are now spreading to disagreements over defence, foreign policy, environmental policy and the whole gamut of governmental issues. The tensions will broaden, they will become more persistent, and they will come to infect every part of the relationship between the emerging European super-state, on the one hand, and the powerful US, on the other. US policy-makers will come to see that dialling one number for Europe may simply result in a whole series of disagreeable phone calls. Forcing the EU countries into a premature or unwanted unity may be bad not only for the European countries themselves, but also for the conduct of US foreign policy as well.

In particular, the US would be well advised to realise that the special relationship between the US and the UK has served both countries well in the post-war period, and still has a great deal to offer. The EU, without the UK as an important economic region is a much weaker body than the EU which has annexed and incorporated the UK within it. A world in which the UK is still free to speak its mind and to support the US when it sees fit is a better place for the US than a world in which the British voice has been silenced and has become part of a consensus view in Fortress Europe. There are not that many powerful national voices in the world that speak up for freedom of speech, democracy, enterprise and liberty. The UK is one of the most prominent after the US. It is in US interests that Britain's voice should not be silenced, just as much as it is in Britain's interest to keep that voice and to make sure it is heard loud and clear in the five continents of the world.

7
What's in an English-Speaking Union for the US?

Should the UK join NAFTA?

During the first weekend of July 2000, a group of US Republican senators arrived in the UK to talk about possible British membership of the North American Free Trade Agreement. A number of contacts had been made over the years between British Conservatives and US Republicans with this in mind. The quickening of the pace represented by the delegation led by Phil Gramm, a senior high-ranking senator, was doubly important. They came during the throes of a presidential election when Republicans confidently expected Governor George W. Bush to win as a Republican. They spoke for the majority of Republicans in the Senate and Congress. They shared a common vision with British Conservatives of the type of world they wished to create. It was doubly exciting for British Conservatives as it offered an alternative to the model of ever-increasing European integration, bigger and dearer government from Brussels, and less and less control over our own destiny that has been dominating British foreign policy for so long.

The North American free trade area has not been without its problems at birth, but it is now progressing well. When it was first constructed between the US and Canada, there were many in Canada who feared a US takeover. They have been pleasantly surprised. It has made trade and friendly contact between Canada and the US easier, but Canada is still a self-governing democracy capable of making its own decisions about foreign policy, taxation, and all the other important matters that constitute a political nation. There were even bigger fears amongst many in the US when NAFTA's doors were opened to the south, to Mexico. There had been long-running battles over the permeable southern US borders as more and more Mexicans migrated to the riches of their northern neighbour. But now many in the US would agree that offering Mexico the hand of friendship and more liberal trade was a good way to stimulate the Mexican economy. In the end, most Americans realised that the only thing which will slow the steady drift of economic migrants north from Mexico to the US is a more prosperous and successful Mexico. NAFTA represents the most positive way for the US to assist Mexico to greater prosperity and higher living standards.

The idea behind the North American Free Trade Agreement is very different from the way the EU idea has evolved. It is a free trade area, rather than a customs union. Its aim is not to create new barriers against the rest of the world in the way that the EU has done through its agricultural and commercial policies, but to reduce the barriers of trade between the members even more rapidly than the barriers to trade are being removed globally through the World Trade Organization. It is an institution hostile to tariff and subsidy. It is based upon the proposition that no government impediment should be placed in the way of a fair and free trade between friendly peoples. It is demonstrating that trade and friendship are solvents of disagreement and political conflict. People are much more reluctant to row if they feel good business will be lost as a result.

The logic of a free trade area is to keep on expanding. It is not an aggressive, imperial operation. It is not a real threat to anyone, and the mood of the world is shifting to see that free trade is an offer and an opportunity rather than a damaging attack on people's way of life. Now that the US is more comfortable with its free trade area with its two nearest neighbours, Canada and Mexico, it is casting its eyes further afield to see who else might be suitable for membership of this exciting project. It has the advantage to Americans of being primarily a US idea. It is not so threatening to the US as it does not curtail its sovereignty in any way that matters to it. It gently expands the US sphere of influence, but mainly through improved contacts, private sector to private sector, which goes with the grain of much US thinking. It is an idea whose time has come, and an idea that the UK should take seriously.

The origins of US enthusiasm to extend free trade to selected countries are varied. The most important point in Washington to date and in US political psychology is the fear that the US has of too much control or intervention from supranational bodies. It may seem surprising to a British audience to learn that exactly the fears that many people legitimately have in Britain about control of their own destiny passing to unelected bureaucracies in Brussels are mirrored by debates in the US about some of the powers of the mighty and sovereign US passing to bureaucratic bodies like the UN, the World Bank, UNESCO and world environmental conferences. The US finds it particularly difficult to accept controls over its policy or freedom of action from others as in the twentieth century it became accustomed to being the most important power in the world, and was able on many occasions to have its own way. US concepts of liberty are bound up with being a successful country economically and politically. Many Americans take the view that the US is pumping out so much cash to support and help countries around the world, it is a bit rich if those same countries then seek to combine through world bodies to impose what to US eyes are unreasonable restrictions on US action.

The paradox is the greater because the US was a crucial founding member of most of the bodies it now has most trouble in dealing with. To British eyes, the constitutions of bodies like the UN, the World Bank and the IMF are carefully drawn as part of the post-war settlement to avoid making unreasonable incursions into the freedom of action of successful countries. The US and the UK were important architects and authors of the post-war supranational institutions, and they are very keen to defend the individual liberties and democracies of the member states that first constituted them. The veto was built in for Security Council members at the UN. No one has ever suggested that the US should have to accept a programme of economic policy laid down by the IMF or World Bank, as the US has never been in a position where it needed to beg favours from those organisations.

Nonetheless, there is a real and understandable worry in the US that transferring too much power to supranational bodies would bode ill for the successful conduct of US foreign policy and the successful upholding of the Anglo-Saxon virtues of liberty, free trade and democracy. An important part of the background to the development of NAFTA is to find an international route forward which leaves countries free to make their own decisions and to place their own bets. Even so, some in the US bridle at the modest international requirements of a free trade area.

The second important point in the US background is the backlash against the world's largest power and the world's policeman. In the post-war period there has been a lot of resentment of US success in many parts of the globe. There has been studied ambivalence on the part of many countries. They resent both the strength of US arms and the strength and depth of the US economy, but when in trouble they often call upon the US to intervene or assist. There have been calls from the Middle East for US mediation, US intervention and US military support during the various conflicts between the Arab states and Israel, and in the individual conflicts between different Arab states. In the Far East, Taiwan needs US support against the imperial ambitions of China. China and Japan compete for the attention and support of the US, whilst China from time to time expresses enormous hostility about any US intervention in Asia. In South America, US money, influence and ideas are regularly sought as juntas and democracies jostle with each other and vie for supremacy. In Europe, many of the countries on the continent expect the US nuclear shield and the promise of US conventional forces in the event of problems to be ever-present, although many of those same continental countries are often damning in their comments on US policy and ideals.

The US has, in recent years, been remarkably even-tempered as many Lilliputian dictatorships and unpleasant regimes around the world have tried to tie the giant down. In many parts of the political establishment in the US, there is an understanding that there can be some future as well as past meaning to the phrase 'the special relationship' between the UK and the US because of this shared experience of being a first power in the world.

Successive British governments after the Suez problems have responded to this by being sympathetic on the whole to the US cause, and offering substantial moral and political support to the US in its chosen courses of action. As we have seen, the special relationship still brings something to both parties.

The idea of offering the UK potential membership of NAFTA is a sign of US Republicans recognising the importance of the special relationship and offering to British Conservatives something that could be very useful to us at a time of decision for the UK. Both believe that British membership of NAFTA would help Britain further to develop its prosperity and economic strength. Both, more importantly, see that it would be a very important gesture to the world, showing that the US and Britain have a lot in common. We should do more things together. It would reinforce the union we have achieved on defence and wider political matters through our joint stance at the UN and our membership of NATO, with an economic grouping based upon principles that together we hold dear.

Many Americans have anglophile leanings, or wish to learn and understand more of the English past. Whilst the US has been successful in creating a cohesive and distinctive culture and a sense of political union out of divergent peoples that came to settle in an important part of the North American continent, many of those peoples are conscious that they are comparatively recent arrivals in a relatively new nation. They do go in search of their origins and seek to understand how their history as an independent country grew directly out of the squabbles and tensions of European settlers and out of the fundamental disagreement between those European settlers and the old home country. Whilst there are now many Spanish-speaking, Italian and Middle European settlers in the US as well, who look to somewhat different cultural and political origins, they are all interested, to some extent, in their English and British background because it had such a decisive impact upon the form, structure, language and early history of the US.

Senator Gramm confirmed this in his speech on UK membership of NAFTA. Although his ancestors came from the continent of Europe, he is conscious of the English origin of his politics, language and the culture of his nation. He values and believes in the English legacy.

US tourists come in their millions to the shores of the UK. They do not come to see 'cool Britannia', or even to celebrate the Beatles. We are not likely to see many of them making the journey to see the new architecture of Docklands, or visiting Liverpool. They come to see the great heritage buildings of the UK. They wish to see the Palace of Westminster to understand the origins of their own democratic system and their own common law. St Paul's Cathedral is of more interest to them than Canary Wharf. They wish to see the castles and palaces and great cathedrals scattered around the country, and to marvel at how people lived before any white man settled in the US. For all US people, there is a historical purpose in coming to the UK. For those who are the direct descendants of the original English settlers, especially the direct descendants of the Puritan Fathers who founded New England, there is a pull on the heart strings as they look at the half-timbered houses, castles and old manor houses inhabited by people at the time that the Puritan rebels set sail on the *Mayflower*.

Similarly, they are fascinated to compare the remains of eighteenth-century London and the great eighteenth-century houses out in the country with what they can see for themselves of the colonial style of architecture developed to such perfection by the men who launched the American War of Independence. Washington and Jefferson were quintessentially English gentlemen abroad. They were educated along English lines, thought the same thoughts, and used the same language to great effect. They were born of the same legal and political tradition. It was their vision of how the colonies needed representation and freedom as much as the home country that led to the ringing words of the Declaration of Independence and the development of a federal constitution for an unruly emerging country.

This shared history is important in creating a climate in which many in the US would like to reinforce rather than diminish the links between the two countries. The War of Independence produced surprisingly little bitterness, as it was out of character with the relationship that has come to dominate in the last 150 years. The UK soon got over the loss of the colonies, recognising the US's right to self-government, and marvelling at the achievements of the US people as they explored and traversed the great continent and then settled it, turning it into an economic empire. On the US side, there could be forgiveness because it won and went on to make such a success of its independence. The American War of Independence is now the subject of the occasional joke when British people meet Americans. There is none of the awkwardness and difficulty that still characterises some meetings of British people with representatives of countries on the continent who have been at war with us in more recent times.

The traditional reason why modern US politicians are interested in developing the British alliance through NAFTA lies in their understanding of the need to win over hearts and minds around the world, rather than simply trying to assert US power. In the post-war period the most searing experience on the US political psyche was that of Vietnam. Many Americans felt that, given the colossal economic strength of the United States and its preparedness to spend a large amount of effort, money and men on the battle against communism, it was only a matter of time before they succeeded in Vietnam. It came as a huge shock to the US that, despite the depressing run of body bags coming home, it was unable to defeat North Vietnam in open battle or guerrilla warfare. It came as an even bigger shock when it was finally forced out of South Vietnam altogether, defeated by what on paper looked to be a rather small and unimportant power with a backward economy. As the US mulled over the consequences of the defeat and tried to learn lessons from what had happened, many concluded that the way to beat communism was through a battle of ideas rather than a military exchange on the ground.

Subsequent events proved them right. The great democracies defeated communism without a shot being fired at the end of the 1980s. People in the communist world came to see for themselves that they were falling further and further behind the West in quality of life and prosperity. They at last also grasped that if enough of them wanted the collapse of the evil empires, then the evil empires would be no more. Winning hearts and minds has become more important to many thinkers in the US than winning military battles or deploying the fifth, sixth or seventh fleet in the right part of the world. NAFTA is more than a free trade area. It represents a coherent set of ideas on how government, people and economic life should be organised, which is to be exported by the soft sell to more and more countries around the world. The cardinal idea behind the whole operation is that free trade cements friendship and encourages common working, whilst individual trading blocs or nations that follow protectionist agendas are more likely to generate conflict and disagreement with one another.

UK interest in joining NAFTA has of course been reinforced by the way peoples and companies have been operating on both sides of the Atlantic for many years. We have seen elsewhere what a surge there has been in mutual investment in each other's countries and how much common action there now is across the Atlantic through mega-mergers and enterprising links. As this is something that US and

British people wish to do, taking advantage of shared language and common enthusiasm for technology, it is something which politicians could belatedly catch up with by agreeing joint membership of a trade association.

US foreign policy towards the EEC, now the EU, is often argued as a reason against developing the NAFTA idea any further. It is true that on a fairly consistent basis, both Republican and Democratic presidents have seemed to favour the idea of closer European integration. The bureaucratic mind thinks it would be much tidier in trying to reach agreement on common action, or a united political stance, if they only had to ring the office of the president of Europe from the office of the US president, and sort it out in a few minutes over the phone. Instead, at the moment, the US president has to consult a series of leading allies, including Britain, France and Germany, on every major issue on which he wishes to progress. Whilst Ronald Reagan was sympathetic to Margaret Thatcher, and seemed to understand some of her difficulties with deeper European integration, George Bush was more guided by the policy establishment at the State Department and often applied subtle pressure on Britain to move closer to our European partners. This pressure has been intensified by President Clinton, probably encouraged by Prime Minister Blair, in the hope that the British people will be swayed to more European integration if we think our US neighbours, friends and relatives are of a similar view.

What is interesting is that the Bush advisers, having had time to think about events after leaving office, came round to the opinion that they had been wrong to advise in favour of closer European integration for Britain. It may well be the case that some of Clinton's advisers come to that conclusion after they leave office as well. The US faces a fundamental dilemma in its policy approach to Europe and the EU. Whilst it sees the advantage of getting Europe to do more for itself and of simplifying the number of people and the range of governments it has to consult when trying to get common action, it also begins to see the threat of creating an EU not in its own image, which could be an unfriendly competitor on the world stage.

The US comes across the EU most often and most actively in the area of trade. It now has a formidable range of cases to prove that the EU is often obstructive, protectionist and combative. The EU would say the same of the US.

Dial one number for Europe?

What America would really like is to be able to dial one number for Europe and to find at the other end of the phone a US voice agreeing with US philosophy and policies. US politicians and policy-makers are at last realising that this is the one thing that cannot be achieved. Some had naively hoped that if Britain plunged in more wholeheartedly to EU, it would mysteriously influence policy in a pro-American direction, and all would be well in the end. These people are now coming to see that European union is driven by Franco-German ideas and political weight, and that if Britain went along with it, it would be unlikely to be able to drag it back to belief in NATO and free trade along the lines that the US seeks. Others now see that having a Britain capable of forming an independent foreign and defence policy, and still in charge of most of its own economic affairs, gives the US a better chance. Geographically, the UK is several steps out into the Atlantic. Morally, politically and philosophically, it is probably mid-Atlantic, with European and US influences and leanings. There have been times in the past when Britain has acted as an honest broker between US and EU views. Many US strategists would now be reluctant to lose this helpful intermediation and are coming to understand that asking Britain to submerge itself in a centralised European union would break that link and remove that opportunity.

The US has not been very impressed by the foreign policy actions of the EU to date. It has seen how EU recognition of Croatia made the problems of a simmering Yugoslavia boil over. The US is learning by bitter experience that the EU is neither ready nor capable of making a decisive difference on the international stage. It is also learning that the slumbering giant of the EU is quite capable of putting its foot in it, but then does not have the capability to rescue or redeem the position.

US ambivalence to a military role for the EU has really been settled in US minds in favour of asking European states to make a bigger contribution to and through NATO, but being hostile to an independent military position by the emerging super-state. If the US had been serious about wanting European countries to take on their own defence without US support, they would, at the end of the Cold War, have issued a timetable or ultimatum for the full withdrawal of US troops, back-up and support, giving perhaps the European countries a ten-year period to recruit and equip sufficiently to take on the task for themselves. Many of us are very glad that the US did not take this view, although we would have understood it, given the hostility expressed – particularly in France – towards many US ideas and much US support. Those of us who favour a stronger and deeper US alliance believe that NATO is a model of how it can be achieved, and we are enthusiastic to keep NATO in being and grateful to the US for the military capability and technology it supplies to guarantee the freedom of the European countries. There is common ground across the Atlantic as US policy has fallen short of insisting that the Europeans spend more and take on more responsibility for themselves. It is important that we do not allow the EU to drive a wedge between the important NATO partners, the UK and the US, as the world would be a less safe place if they did so.

All these things in the US psyche impel many in the US to see the need for closer links with countries like the UK. The idea of extending NAFTA is not just to create an English-speaking alliance, although that will have the most impact when it extends beyond trade and commerce to foreign policy and defence. The idea of the economic alliance through NAFTA is to extend it as an opportunity to any country that wishes to join, and can meet the qualifying requirements. Unlike the EU, where once you have joined you are then put under more and more pressure to mend your ways and change your laws as the EU goes through a period of continuous revolution, in the case of joining NAFTA, once you have met the qualifying requirements no additional requirements will be imposed upon the member states. In the case of the EU, there is no clause in the treaty enabling a member state to leave if it has changed its mind, whereas in the case of NAFTA, countries are free to join and leave as they see fit. It is a voluntary association of like-minded states that have shown their like-mindedness by the policies they have followed.

NAFTA

The overarching idea behind NAFTA is to promote the freest possible trade between those countries that believe in free trade. Belief in free trade extends to belief in keeping the demands of government to a modest level. It means that to qualify, countries have to show that they have law codes and tax regimes that leave people and companies as free as possible. In Washington they draw up an index of economic liberalism. Countries like Chile and the UK score rather well, as a result of the exciting market-oriented policies followed in both countries in the 1980s and 1990s. The idea is to use NAFTA as a magnet to attract countries to its prosperity and success and to encourage them, by that success, to understand the economic and commercial policies that underpin it.

The US–Canada agreement

The US and Canada entered a free trade agreement in 1989. The full North America Free Trade Agreement was signed by Canadian, Mexican and US representatives in December 1992, and the area came into effect on 1 January 1994. The objectives of the Agreement were stated clearly at the beginning of the document:

(a) eliminate barriers to trade in, and facilitate the cross-border movement of, goods and services between the territories of the parties;

(b) promote conditions of fair competition in the free trade area;

(c) increase substantially investment opportunities in the territories of the parties;

(d) provide adequate and effective protection and enforcement of intellectual property rights in each party's territory;

(e) create effective procedures for the implementation and application of this agreement, for its joint administration and for the resolution of disputes; and

(f) establish a framework for further trilateral, regional and multilateral co-operation to expand and enhance the benefits of this Agreement.

The general provisions entailed the reduction of tariffs over a 15-year period, with the exact timetable varying from sector to sector. Investment restrictions were lifted in most sectors, allowing companies in one country to invest in another with the exception of oil in Mexico, culture in Canada, and airline and radio communications in the US. Any of the signatory countries can leave the treaty with six months' notice, and the treaty allows for the inclusion of new members. Government procurement is opened up over a period of ten years, gradually eliminating the areas where a country like

Mexico reserves contracts for Mexican competitors only. Panels of independent arbitrators were established to resolve disagreements arising out of the treaty.

Two side agreements were included at the insistence of President Clinton, who needed them to gain acceptance of the provisions of the treaty in the US. The first is on the environment, and the second is to guarantee minimum standards of treatment of employees in the labour market. From the year 2000, North American trucks can drive anywhere in the three countries without economic restriction. Mexico is gradually opening its financial sector to US and Canadian investment, eliminating all the barriers by 2007. Tariffs on cars are removed over a five-year period where any car for which local content exceeds 62.5 per cent is free from tariffs. The US and Mexico set up a North American Development Bank to help finance the clean-up of the US/Mexican border. The treaty itself is very detailed, tackling third-country dumping, rules of origin, customs procedures, import and export restrictions, export taxes, technical barriers to trade, government procurement, investment services and related matters, telecommunications, competition policy, financial services, intellectual property, and all other relevant issues governing a complex trade in goods, services, investment and intellectual property between three sophisticated trading economies.

How NAFTA works

NAFTA is run by a commission and secretariat. Commissioners are empowered to call on technical advisers, to create working groups or expert groups as they see fit. Individual complainants can also request an arbitral panel. The three countries concerned maintain a roster of up to thirty individuals who are willing and able to serve as panellists. The roster members are appointed by consensus for terms of three years and may be reappointed. When there are two parties to a dispute, a panel is established of five members; two chosen by each side and a chairman selected by agreement. The two panellists chosen have to be citizens of the other country. After hearing evidence and going through the proper procedures, the panel presents a final report which the disputing parties are expected to accept and to comply with.

NAFTA is run by a series of committees. There is a committee on trade in goods, a committee on trade in worn clothing, a committee on agricultural trade, a committee on sanitary and phytosanitary measures, a committee on standards-related measures, a committee on small business, a financial services committee and an advisory committee on private commercial disputes. Article 2202 makes it quite clear that any country or group of countries may accede to the NAFTA agreement subject to satisfactory negotiations with NAFTA.

NAFTA is an example of a fairly open voluntary agreement. Members consent to an enforcement procedure to make sure that the agreement is seen through, but there is no supranational apparatus with a law court asserting itself above the individual member states as there is in the EU. Whereas the EU is a customs union, with substantial government apparatus on top, NAFTA is a genuinely free trade area whose main purpose is to lower tariff and non-tariff barriers to trade. If Britain were to join NAFTA, there would be no problem for the other NAFTA members, but Britain would have to secure from its EU partners agreement to cease levying the common external tariff on US, Canadian and Mexican products that would still be levied in the other member states of the EU. The difficulty some people have with the concept of dual membership of the EU and NAFTA for the UK shows how different a free market like NAFTA is from a constrained and protected market like the EU. Many people in Britain wrongly think that the single market, or common market, is also a free market, whereas it has more of the characteristics of a customs union with a number of laws and interventions by the European government to control the market and to keep out foreign competition.

Looking around the world, it is often the English-speaking countries that would find it easiest to qualify under the NAFTA rules. Countries like New Zealand and Australia, in common with the UK, have law codes and tax regimes that are friendlier to business activity than many of the more restrictive and higher tax regimes that we see on the continent of Europe. It is easier for English-speaking countries to be influenced by US culture, media and success, and in turn to wish to follow some US policies which underpin that success.

Belonging to NAFTA does not prevent people belonging to other alliances and bodies in the world. It does not produce any conflict with membership of the Security Council of the United Nations, nor, for that matter, with membership of the EU all the time that that, too, is wedded to removing barriers to trade within the EU area. The question most in debate in the UK is whether it is feasible for the UK to join NAFTA at the same time as belonging to the EU itself. There are four different positions argued by the protagonists in this debate.

1. First of all there is the position taken by the Labour government and many of its supporters that membership of NAFTA is impossible and undesirable. They have a fear of belonging to a body with so much US influence, and they are not philosophically well disposed towards the underlying principles which state clearly that you do not attempt to protect ailing businesses and failing industries, and you do believe that keeping the burdens of government light is the best way to create jobs and prosperity. Whilst many of these Labour supporters will accept clauses in the EU treaty, banning industrial subsidy and that type of protection within the European area, their conversion to these beliefs is at best skin-deep, as they do not wish to apply them more generally through the NAFTA area. Some in the Foreign Office believe that under the Treaty of Rome and subsequent amendments, the UK has no power or right to negotiate its own trade relationships with countries outside the EU. Asking the EU to do it for us, in the Foreign Office's view, is not likely to be successful or productive.

2. The second position is that adopted by some Conservatives, that we should try to persuade the EU as a whole to join NAFTA. There are obvious advantages in this. If it makes sense to have a free trade area extending over the North American continent, and if it makes sense to have a single market extending over much of the European continent, surely it would make sense to put the two together? There are two problems to be overcome. The first is that many of our European partners would allow their anti-American prejudices to come to the fore, and would not be enthusiastic about this proposal. It is likely that France would organise a resistance to any suggestion that the whole of the European single market should be joined with the North American free trade area in a large free trade system. The second problem is that many of the European countries would be hard-pushed to fulfil the letter and spirit of the NAFTA rules, as they still maintain substantial protectionist elements in their individual and common policies through the EU Common Agricultural Policy (CAP) and the EU's rather selective approach to controlling industrial subsidy and

intervention. It would be worth a try – and, were it possible to pull off this diplomatic coup, then of course the rules of NAFTA would become some kind of restraint on the wrong kind of policies being followed by some EU states. There is no direct conflict between the ideas of NAFTA and the free market strands in the European treaties. The problem rests in the selective interpretation and enforcement of the European treaties, meaning that in many parts of the Union there are still unacceptable protectionist measures which are not being properly controlled by Brussels or the European Court. The terms of the EU/Mexico Trade Agreement in March 2000 show that progress can be made in this field by the whole EU.

3. The third position is that it would be better for Britain to belong to NAFTA than to the EU, and that we should choose between the two. Given that NAFTA is a looser kind of association without a massive joining fee and subscription – one has to pay to belong to the EU – and given that NAFTA is based on the principles of allowing sovereign countries to make their own decisions, there is a growing body of opinion in Britain which thinks that this would be more compatible with the attitudes and genius of the British people than with the EU as it is evolving. Those who favour strengthening our links with Europe see this as the only honest position with respect to NAFTA. They are deliberately trying to make it an either–or choice as part of their political strategy of branding anyone who wants a different kind of European Union from the French and German model as being someone who in practice wants us to leave altogether.

4. The fourth position is that we should use the very considerable negotiating power we have during a period of renegotiating the treaties to get ourselves the opportunity to join NAFTA, even if the others do not wish to do so. I see nothing incompatible for Britain in belonging both to NAFTA and to the single market of Europe. I think it would be quite possible to negotiate that, as I have never taken the view that our partners really want to get rid of us from the whole operation. They would be extremely foolish to want to forgo the substantial British financial contribution, and they would at once appreciate that as they sell us so much more than we sell them, they have a lot more at risk. Of course, it would require considerable political will and diplomatic skill on Britain's

part to do this. There would be interesting problems with the CAP, but as we are committed to reform of the agricultural policy anyway, that, too, could be a proper matter for negotiation on both sides of the Atlantic. It could be that such a negotiation proves the trigger for tackling the rather intractable problems of agricultural protection on both sides of the Atlantic at the same time. It is certainly the case that we would be able to join NAFTA despite belonging to the CAP, given the very different way agriculture is treated in all of the jurisdictions concerned. We would need our partners' agreement to lowering the EU tariff on US goods into the UK. The EU negotiation of a Free Trade Agreement with Mexico shows that there are ways forward in bringing the two blocs closer together. Its success should give heart to British negotiators seeking a new relationship with NAFTA.

A Britain which was allowed by our partners to join NAFTA as well would also be a Britain that had decided to opt out of the further round of centralisation and integration on the continent. It would be a Britain much happier with itself, feeling that its instincts and ambitions had been better understood on both sides of the Atlantic. We would be in Europe but not run by it, in the words of the Conservative slogan. We would be a full part of the single market and a strong voice for its growing liberalisation, whilst at the same time being a leading member of NAFTA, wishing to take the NAFTA message to other parts of the world. Whilst countries like Chile may well join NAFTA and add a strong Spanish-speaking element to the Mexican contingent already in the organisation, the most likely future candidates of NAFTA are English-speaking countries. Churchill's vision of an ultimate English-speaking union would be one step nearer in the economic sphere if Britain joined NAFTA and was followed by other leading English-speaking countries.

The US has a lot to gain from this strategy. The world is changing a lot. The dot.com revolution is creating a world of networks and informal links. People in the US are getting tired of the heavy, bureaucratic, centralised institutions set up in the immediate post-war world, and are becoming frustrated at the way in which bringing in so many countries to these organisations for good reasons can slow down their decision-making, or alter their decision-making in a way that is not compatible with US aims and ideals. When you get to such a position, the best course of action is to do something new, something exciting and invigorating. NAFTA is an idea whose time has come. It would give a new impetus to economic progress, it would tie in with the spirit of the internet age, and it would bring English-speaking peoples closer together in a wholly desirable way.

The loneliness of the long-distance great power would be eased somewhat by having more friends and allies in an economic linking with the US, to supplement and complement the strength of the alliance on defence and foreign policy through NATO. The US has not always been well served by some of its NATO partners, but the structure of NATO has held because it does not force countries to do things they do not wish to do. NAFTA is a similarly strong but flexible structure which is more exciting, and more likely to survive, than the highly centralised structure which France and Germany wish to superimpose upon the EU.

The US will not, for the foreseeable future, be able to dial one number for Europe and get a European president on the end of the phone who can speak for all countries. It will certainly never be able to dial one number for Europe and get a European president on the phone who agrees with it. One of the least desirable characteristics of continental debate is the virulent brand of anti-Americanism which we see emerging at certain times over certain issues. Britain joining NAFTA would mean that we could continue our pivotal role in acting as a bridge across the Atlantic, an interpreter of the US to the continent, and the continent to the US. It does not mean we would become a US poodle any more than we would wish to be the poodle of the Franco-German alliance. Britain is a sizeable and important independent country still, whose weight could be important on commercial matters through NAFTA and on some single market matters through the EU.

The US and Britain intuitively understand that in this fast-moving, technologically driven internet-based world, the peoples and countries that will do best are the ones that control the demands of government, keep their law codes flexible and light, and keep their taxes down. Not all of our partners on the continent have understood this, and those who have understood it find it difficult or impossible to practice it. That is why it would be good for Britain and good for the US to make a blow for freedom by linking our trading patterns through NAFTA to supplement our current system of networks and alliances.

8
What Kind of Renegotiation with the EU does Britain Want?

How feasible is renegotiation?

In the previous chapter I have set out to demonstrate that the Eurocentric foreign policy pursued by the UK in the post-war period has been bad for Britain and not particularly good for our continental colleagues. We have been an unhappy partner. Many on the continent have seen us as a sheet anchor, dragging the ship of European integration backwards, or trying to slow it down as often as possible. Some people in Britain have grown impatient with the government's indecision over Europe because they wish to join more wholeheartedly in the schemes of European union and integration. Many others have grown despondent, seeing successive administrations claiming that all we want is a glorified free trade area, but being dragged ineluctably into something much bigger and deeper.

The EU is in a state of perpetual flux or renegotiation. In the current British debate there is a polarised and unenlightening argument between those who say that we need to renegotiate our entry and those who claim that all renegotiation is tantamount to saying we wish to leave the Union in its entirety. Any independent analysis of the current state of the EU would conclude that it is always possible to renegotiate, and that most of the partners most of the time, led by the Commission, are constantly striving to renegotiate the founding treaties. There is very rarely a pause of longer than a year between one treaty and another. The ink is not normally dry on one treaty before people are talking about what should be in the next one. Like a regular bus service, if you miss the first bus there will be another along quickly.

Perhaps what people have in mind when they say that renegotiation is either impossible or tantamount to exit is their realisation that the aims of many in Britain who wish to renegotiate the treaty more in our own image are unrealistic in relation to what our other partners are seeking. The very same people who argue that Europe is going our way are the ones who claim that if we try to confirm it is going our way by putting the relevant clauses in the treaty, we are somehow upping sticks, taking our bat away and ceasing to play the game. Indeed, some of those who are keenest on more European integration seem to hold the dimmest view of our European partners. Those of us who wish to renegotiate a better deal for Britain are constantly told that if we try to do so they will stop trading with us, impose sanctions on us, or even throw us out of the club. There is no legal power under the treaty to do any of these things, our trading ability is protected by international law as well as European law, and the fact that the other European countries sell us rather more than we sell them doesn't seem to worry those who argue we must join in. They believe that if Britain provokes the Community too far by seeking something different from the other members, we will be turned from pariah to former member quite quickly.

As this book is being written, final touches are being made to the Treaty of Nice. Before negotiations on Nice were far advanced in the midsummer of 2000, the French and German governments were already holding private and public meetings to drive forward the idea of yet another treaty to create a constitution for the new Europe. Popular in their debate now is to create an inner core of countries which presses on to the ultimate goal of political union. They are becoming worried that they might be held up not just by Britain, but by some of the more reluctant Scandinavian countries and the new applicant countries coming in who will be some way away from being able to accept all the requirements of the Union as it stands or the union as they wish it to develop.

It is against this background of permanent revolution or renegotiation that the UK needs to make a stand for what it believes in.

The Treaty of Nice

The draft Treaty of Nice is game, set and match for those who wish to create a centralised United States of Europe. Billed as the leftovers from Amsterdam, the British government has been trying to play the whole thing down in its usual way. Yet any analysis of the significance of the draft proposals shows that the Commission, the European Court of Justice (ECJ) and the European Parliament are once again out to increase their power dramatically.

The treaty designed by the Commission plans to make some fundamental breakthroughs in increasing the power and jurisdiction of the European institutions. Their first objective is to underwrite the supremacy of Community law in all respects. A series of court cases, treaty amendments and treaty interpretations has left us in a position where it is commonly thought that the ECJ is the only supreme court operating in the UK. It is the one court that has the power to make or break laws passed by the British Parliament, adjudicating whether they are in line with European law or not. This treaty is designed to reinforce that position and to make sure that all British courts are subservient to the ultimate jurisdiction of the ECJ and the supremacy of European law.

The second area of major advance is in the field of taxation. The Community wishes to establish its right to tax citizens of the United States of Europe wherever they may be resident. A Commission working paper produces five major areas where it wishes to proceed to common Community taxation based on majority voting. Whilst the British government and the Commission persevere with the cover story that the most important taxation issues are subject to unanimity giving the British a right to say 'No', the areas identified in the Commission working document for qualified majority voting would drive a coach and horses through much of the British veto.

The third big area of advance lies in the proposal to change qualified majority voting itself. The Commission has proposed a double simple majority system to replace the current qualified or weighted majority. If the Commission could secure a simple majority of member states and that simple majority also reflected a simple majority of the population of the EU, then the measure passes. This substantially dilutes the current qualified majority voting threshold.

The fourth area of advance is in strengthening the powers of the European Parliament which is offered co-decision in a wider range of areas. The power of the president of the Commission is to be stronger. The president would gain the power to fire individual Commissioners that he or she did not like.

The fifth area is in the weakening of the link between member states and representation on the various institutions of the Community. It is quite likely that the provision that every member state has a representative judge at the ECJ would be broken. It is quite likely that there will be fewer Commissioners than there are member states. Whatever happens, Britain will lose one of its current two European Commissioners, and could lose the second from time to time as well. The number of MEPs is to be limited to the current level of 700 and the preferred solution is to introduce 10 per cent of the MEPs elected from trans-European lists. As new member states join, this means a substantial reduction in the number of MEPs for any individual country.

A great deal of power has already passed from Britain to the European institutions through successive treaties – the Treaty of Rome, the Single European Act, the Treaty of Maastricht once the opt-outs have been removed, the Treaty of Amsterdam and now the proposed Treaty of Nice. Each one of these treaties has been presented as a series of minor amendments that should not scare the British people. Taken together they represent a huge transfer of power. The draft Treaty of Nice is the most federal of them all, completing the process, transferring more and more power to a centralised government in Brussels and the European Parliament.

We must ask the British people whether this is what they had in mind when they voted 'Yes' to a Common Market in 1975? Is it right to transfer so much power to a group of people and institutions that have not been known either for their honest dealing or their democratic ways? Should the people who have given us the Common Agricultural Policy and the Common Fisheries Policy be entrusted with a Common Economic Policy, Common Criminal Policy and much else besides? Wouldn't it be better if the EU tried to do well in those areas where it already has wide-ranging power, like agriculture and fishing, before being trusted with many new responsibilities? The British negotiating position should be the preservation of unanimity on tax matters and the refusal to countenance any more qualified majority voting at the expense of our veto on other issues. If we sign the full Treaty of Nice we sign the death warrant of an independent democracy in Britain. If we sign the draft Treaty of Nice we are on a slippery slope to common taxation. If we sign the Treaty of Nice we are transferring a large number of decisions away from our democracy to their bureaucracy. The EU has not solved the democratic deficit. The democratic deficit will be made worse if more powers are transferred away from national parliaments. The democratic deficit would be reduced if instead the Treaty of Nice transferred some powers that Europe has taken but not used to good effect back to the member states. Many British people share my worry about losing more control over important questions in our national life.

A Nice rollercoaster to common taxation

The Commission paper on taxation and social security measures is complicated and understated. It is all part of creating a super-state by stealth. The Commission sets out a series of areas where qualified majority voting should be introduced. The first of these is to coordinate provisions intending to remove direct obstacles to the exercise of the four freedoms, the freedom of movement of people, capital, goods and services. This is a wide-ranging exemption from unanimity, although the Commission is careful to try to play down its significance. Draft Article 93 states:

> measures for the co-ordination of provisions laid down by law, regulation or administrative action in Member States in order to remove direct obstacles to the free movement of goods, persons, services or capital arising from tax provisions and in particular to prevent discrimination and double taxation.

Which should proceed by majority vote.

Second, the Commission recommends qualified majority voting (QMV) for measures which modernise and simplify the Community rules in the direct tax area in order to eliminate evasion and fraud.

> measures for the co-ordination of provisions laid down by law, regulation or administrative action in Member States concerning direct taxation in order to prevent fraud, evasion or tax avoidance.

Third, QMV is to be introduced for measures which ensure a uniform application of existing indirect taxation rules and guarantees a simple and transparent application of such rules.

> measures concerning value added tax, excise duty and capital duty which modernise or simplify existing Community rules or ensure a uniform application or ensure the simple and transparent application of such rules, other than those which fix the rates of tax or bring about a general change in the system of taxation.

Fourth, unanimity is out for taxation measures which have as their principal objective the protection of the environment and have a direct and significant effect on the environment.

> taxation measures which have as their principal objective the pursuit of the environmental objectives of the Treaty such as laid down in particular in Article 174, and have a direct and significant effect on the environment.

Fifth, provisions aimed at prevent fraud, evasion or tax avoidance in order to eliminate cases of double non-taxation in cross-border situations and to prevent circumvention of existing provisions particularly in the VAT field are also to be decided on majority votes.

> measures concerning indirect taxation in order to prevent fraud, evasion or tax avoidance and to prevent circumvention of existing provisions.

These five provisions would allow the EU to impose taxes in Britain even where we had lost the vote on them. The immediate targets the Commission have in mind are the Sulphur Levy and the savings or withholding tax. The Commission explicitly states that the savings or withholding tax is a measure which could go through on QMV under its intended treaty changes concerning the prevention of fraud or double non-taxation. The Climate Change Levy would be a natural choice under the enhanced environmental tax provisions, along with possible taxes on landfill, planning applications and other matters mentioned by the Commission in its document. Whilst the Commission rules out an immediate move towards a common VAT levied as the first Europe-wide tax on the basis of a qualified majority vote, it does intend to use qualified majority voting under this draft treaty to change the VAT rules and to change the incidence of VAT. It cites the kind of problem it wishes to sort out as being the imposition of VAT on letters charged by private mail carriers, alongside the exemption from VAT of public mail monopolies and the exemption from VAT of certain electronic commerce transactions.

Britain has already given in over certain Community tax measures. VAT was introduced at the request of the EEC when Britain joined. There have been endless skirmishes as the original British rate was well below the preferred band for VAT set by the European Community. Britain has also wished to maintain zero-rating on a range of sensitive items, including newspapers, books and children's clothing which the Community would prefer to see taxed. Britain opposed a tax on the art market, but lost, and has now suffered this imposition on the very successful London-based auction houses. As a result, some business has diverted to untaxed markets outside the EU altogether.

The idea behind the Treaty of Nice is to extend the EU's powers of taxation substantially. If some or all of these measures are blocked at Nice, they will reappear in future court judgments and treaty changes. Trying to stop fraud or tax evasion will give the Community a platform for doing almost anything it likes. Trying to create a harmonised marketplace throughout the single market area will give it another pretext for dramatic tax changes over the years. Of course, the EU will play down the significance of the move in the run up to signing the treaty. It has always done so in the past. Once the treaty is signed, then EU officials will make clear what the member states have done. They will begin with some modest proposals along the lines they have originally set out, but will soon move on to more dramatic manifestations of their new tax-creating powers. The EU does wish to create a harmonised system of company taxation, a harmonised system of taxation on savings and investment, and a series of Europe-wide environmental and energy taxes. It wishes to deliver VAT as the first truly European tax imposed by the Union where the money is redistributed to the member states as the Union sees fit. The Treaty of Nice could be a stepping stone on the way to this end result. In due course they will wish to have influence or control over aspects of income tax as well. Once the principle of taxing savings is established, the rest of income is likely to follow.

The EU also wishes to harmonise and to gain greater powers over social security. The draft Treaty of Nice proposes coordination of social security schemes to facilitate the free movement of people, and seeks qualified majority voting over measures providing for minimum requirements which are necessary to allow for the effective exercise of the free movement of people and to prevent distortions of competition through the artificial lowering of social protection standards.

It has long been a bugbear of the EU that some member states pay rather lower social security benefits than others. They know they will never be able to sort this problem out whilst vetoes remain in place, and so the Treaty of Nice proposes removing two of these crucial vetoes to speed up the process of harmonisation. Europe's answer to measures which destroy jobs in some countries is always to export these measures to others rather than remove them from the countries which are badly affected by them.

Draft Article 137 adds to the list of areas where the EU is to proceed with new laws acting by majority vote:

> Social security and social protection of workers; protection of workers where their employment contract is terminated;
> representation and collective defence of the interests of workers and employers, including co-determination, subject to para. 6;
> conditions of employment for third country nationals legally residing in Community territory;
> financial contributions for promotion of employment and job creation, without prejudice to the provisions relating to the Social Fund.

The UK has already surrendered much of its right to independent social and employment policies. The Labour government gave away our veto over Social Chapter proposals. The UK has lost an important court case at the ECJ, requiring us to implement the Working Time Directive even though the British government opposed it and thought it was a matter requiring our consent. This draft treaty will open up the possibility of many employment measures affecting labour relations in Britain, as well as some social security matters, now being settled in Brussels rather than London. The treaty is especially keen to extend higher payments from one country to another and increase the costs of employment EU-wide.

Reform of Community courts

Such is the confidence of the EU that the reform of the Community courts is designed to give more cases under European law to the national courts than they currently enjoy. The EU justice system has been swamped by its own territorial acquisitiveness. It is taking 21 months for a case to come to judgment in the ECJ and 30 months in the Court of First Instance, the court set up by the treaty of Amsterdam to speed the whole process up. More and more cases are having to come to the European courts because European jurisdiction is so much more intrusive. National courts are more and more reluctant to opine on European matters for fear of the European Court taking a different view.

The EU now feels so sure that it has established its supremacy over national courts that it wishes to trust them rather more and to prevent so many appeals from national courts to the ECJ over the interpretation of European law. A centralised system has now been created. The idea is a pyramid, with the ECJ at the top dealing with new points and fundamental issues. The Court of First Instance will take all cases that need a Europe-wide court, including cases involving the European institutions and the member states themselves which were previously preserved to the sole jurisdiction of the ECJ. Most cases will now proceed through the national courts which are under a strict treaty obligation under the Treaty of Nice to enforce the European law. The new Article 234 of the treaty will state in a new Clause 1:

> Subject to the provisions of this Article the Courts and Tribunals of the member states shall rule on questions of Community law which they encounter in exercise of their national jurisdiction.

The ECJ is still there to interpret the treaty and to act as the ultimate source of all authority. Appeals will be rarer and requests for a ruling from the ECJ will be reduced. In future, where a national court wishes to have an ECJ ruling, it will have to specify why the validity or the interpretation of the rule of Community law raises difficulties in the case it is examining.

The intention is to make justice speedier, but it may not make it fairer. The Commission and the European Court are thinking of setting up a series of tribunals for dealing with things like patents with limited rights of appeal to the European Court. They are faced with the conundrum of how to get speedier justice without injustice. Their intention is clear: a strong Community-wide based law where the national courts are subservient to the European Court and where European law covers most of the important issues at stake. The scope for national differentiation and national law-making in democratic fora will be greatly reduced if this reform is introduced in full.

The idea is to bring EU law into line with EU and ECJ wishes. As the Commission states in its proposal:

> In an enlarged Union it will be necessary to safeguard the effectiveness of the Community's judicial system and the consistency of its case law, factors which are essential if Community law is to be applied uniformly in an increasingly diverse Europe. Enlargement will entail an increase in the volume of litigation, not only in quantitative terms but also in qualitative terms as the courts of the new Member States will have to become familiar with Community law.

The Commission is once again being honest in telling us that there will be a big expansion in the amount of EU law, and that all states will have to implement it. Member states' courts will be more tightly controlled, doing more of the work with less and less scope to make their own decisions about the impact of EU law in their country.

An example of the dangers to the UK can be seen in the proposals to govern takeovers at EU level. We may find ourselves in a situation where the UK system based on a Code and the Panel is superseded by an EU system where a tribunal or even the courts interfere. This could damage the market for corporate control quite substantially.

Diluting the qualified majority

Under the current system, a measure going through under qualified majority requires 62 votes cast in favour. Looked at from the negative point of view, it takes 26 votes to block a proposal which the Commission is recommending. There is a total of 87 votes given to the 15 member states (see Table 8.1). The large states – Germany, France, Italy and the United Kingdom – each have ten votes. The smallest state – Luxembourg – has two, and the others are ranged between those two figures. The introduction of Poland, the Czech Republic, the Slovak Republic, Hungary, Slovenia, Romania, Bulgaria, Lithuania, Latvia, Estonia, Malta, Cyprus and Turkey, all potential entrants to the EU, will entail a rapid expansion of the total number of votes and in the number of votes required either to carry an issue or to block it. Clearly the accession of new states does require rethinking the basis of member state voting and the nature of the qualified majority. However, as always the Commission has latched upon the widening or expansion of the Community as an excuse to deepen and strengthen the centralising tendencies.

Table 8.1   Present member states

Member	Population (m)	No. weighted votes	People per vote (m)
Belgium	10.2	5	2.04
Denmark	5.3	3	1.76
Germany	82.0	10	8.20
Greece	10.5	5	2.1
Spain	39.4	8	4.95
France	59.0	10	5.90
Ireland	3.7	3	1.23
Italy	57.6	10	5.76
Luxembourg	0.4	2	0.2
Netherlands	15.8	5	3.16
Austria	8.1	4	2.02
Portugal	10.0	5	2.0
Finland	5.2	3	1.73
Sweden	8.9	4	2.22
UK	59.4	10	5.94
	375.5	87	
Qualified Majority		62	
Blocking Minority		26	

Source: House of Commons Library.

Its proposed solution of double simple majority dilutes the number of votes that would be required to carry any measure. They propose that instead of needing to collect all the votes required under the present qualified majority, as long as those voting represented a majority of the member states and a majority of the population, the matter would carry. This is a significant dilution on certain permutations of votes of the current requirement of the qualified majority. There are currently over seventy treaty articles and sub-articles in the main treaties requiring unanimous voting in the Council of Ministers. The idea of the new Treaty of Nice is to reduce this to twenty only, covering constitutional and a few other matters. In the modern EU, proposals coming forward under qualified majority voting are normally secured. Only the Commission has the right to bring forward such measures. No member state can make its own proposal. If a member state is no longer able to block proposals on its own, it has lost its one remaining important power to influence events.

As Germany, France and Italy together constitute more than half the population of the EU, they can combine with any five other countries under the new system to push a measure through. Under the present system, France, Germany and Italy would need at least six other countries to win a vote, and might need as many as eight other countries depending on which countries are in their alliance. I have assumed in each case that the UK wishes to block the measure. It shows how much more difficult it will prove for the UK to stop things going through. Instead of having to ally with as few as three other countries, the UK would need to find six others hostile to the measure where France and Germany were acting in concert with Italy. It is common for France, Italy and Germany to agree.

Electing MEPs

Perhaps the most radical proposal of all in the document is that about the European Parliament itself. The Commission wishes to have the right to block parties standing for election that the EU does not like. Whilst this is couched in terms of wishing to prevent racism and Nazism reappearing in Europe, it would be most important to make sure that it did not transpose into an antipathy to anti-EU parties who might be expressing a legitimate democratic view which was neither racist nor fascist. In addition, the Commission and the European Parliament wish to see 10 per cent of the MEPs in the first instance elected from trans-European lists. This immediately makes it difficult or impossible for national-based parties to put forward candidates and win seats whilst proposing a distinctively British or French or German point of view. If the existing national parties wish to participate in this contest they are likely to have to form strong alliances on a cross-border basis leading to the construction of a common party platform for the European elections. This is clearly designed to prevent independent national initiative or the expression of different national views on European matters.

There is a strong feeling in parts of the Brussels political establishment that so-called 'Euroscepticism' is not a legitimate political view. If anyone queries the long march to a European super-state, or disagrees with the powers and decisions of the Brussels government, they are portrayed as being outside the pale of decent European opinion. Many of us cannot be happy with a series of self-serving institutions that think they should be immune to criticism. The proposals for the European Parliament are designed to deflect the views of those who are against more European government. The scheme would make it very difficult for good Europeans against more Brussels government to be elected to the European Parliament.

Reforming the other institutions

Two possibilities open up for reforming the Commission in a world of many more member states. The first is that each member state should have its own Commissioner. The second is that the number of Commissioners should be limited so that a member state even as big as the UK would not necessarily have a Commissioner. The absence or presence of a national Commissioner would be organised on a rota basis with each member state having a turn.

Similarly, it is likely that the number of judges in the ECJ will be limited to 13, thereby entailing a break in the link between member states and the ECJ in some cases. There will be similar changes to the Economic and Social Committee.

The impact of the ideas behind the draft Treaty of Nice

The whole draft Treaty of Nice is about the creation of a United States of Europe with a centralised government based on Brussels. Whilst it does give some limited increased power to the European Parliament it is mainly a massive increase in the power of the ECJ and the European Commission. Under the proposals the European Commission president would have the power to sack individual Commissioners. Collective responsibility and unified view would be a necessary prerequisite of holding office and maintaining office. In every area, national interest and national sentiment are to be snuffed out. In every area bar a few constitutional items the veto is to be removed. If they do not secure all they want at Nice, they will be back for more quite soon

Parallel to the work of the Treaty of Nice is work towards an army, navy and air force of the EU and the strengthening of a common foreign policy. Under the Treaty of Amsterdam, Britain is already pledged to loyalty to the common foreign policy and is under a moral obligation to try to help form such a policy. Under the proposals now being discussed things will move rapidly towards the assertion that foreign policy is the prerogative of the EU rather than the member states. That foreign policy will be backed up by some kind of military force or presence.

The draft treaty itself would allow member states wishing to make more rapid progress towards ultimate unity to do so using the powers, the money and the institutions of the EU itself. The EU is not merely impatient with Britain preventing agreement on a number of matters creating a more centralised state, but it now wishes to sweep away the reservations of some of the other states apart from Britain by allowing a central core led by France and Germany to charge ahead to ultimate union.

The biggest weakness of this structure is in its contempt for the democratic process and for national sentiment. Many of us share an antipathy towards crude aggressive nationalism of the kind we saw rampant in Europe in the 1930s. Most of us are reassured there is nothing like this on offer at the moment. Nonetheless, people do still feel French or Italian or British or German and their politicians have not yet persuaded them to replace this primary loyalty with a primary loyalty to Europe. If at the same time the politicians are busily taking powers away from democratic institutions and elected representatives and giving them to unelected officials deliberating in secret around the Brussels conference table, they are creating potentially dangerous precedents.

The very substance of democratic life depends on the consent of the people governed for the institutions and manner of government. The British state has been stable for the past 300 years because there has been that consent to the system. Those who lost the last election still believe in the system that replaces one government with another and know that they have the opportunity to work through the press and the ballot box to seek to overturn the government they do not like. Citizens of the new Europe have no such luxury. They see no direct means of changing the government of Europe which is the Commission. They have absolutely no authority or control over the ECJ which has become the prime mover in creating centralised government on the continent administered through a common law code. The danger of the Treaty of Nice is that it will allow the frustrations to boil over. Democratic politicians in the member states should not sign this treaty. The UK should sound the alarm bells immediately. The Treaty of Nice is a couple of treaties too far. The European peoples are not ready for it. The method of government is not democratic. There will be no consent.

What Britain might seek in a renegotiation?

Given the big erosion of powers of the UK people and Parliament through successive treaties from Rome to Amsterdam and Nice, we need to go back to the basic idea that the British electorate approved in a referendum in 1975. The debate prior to that referendum, and the referendum question itself were quite clear. The British people were asked to vote for a common market. Indeed the words 'common market' appeared in the referendum question. No one in favour of our remaining in the Common Market in that campaign said that we were joining a club about to evolve into an economic, monetary and political union. Speakers in the 'Yes' campaign fell over backwards to assure us that very little power would transfer, that we would remain a sovereign nation with a lively democratic Parliament in charge of most things. They were keen to scotch any rumours of a United States of Europe emerging with an army, a common economic policy, a common foreign policy, common policing, and its own criminal law code. Nothing was further from the minds of those who advocated 'Yes', and nothing was further from the minds of the British people when, by a big majority, they voted 'Yes' to remain in that Common Market.

Any renegotiation should take it as a given that the British people knowingly voted for a common market and, judging by recent opinion polls, would do so again if a simple common market were on offer without all the other trappings of a super-state being attached.

In order to recreate this state of grace the British negotiators would need to set out the following propositions.

First, we should state that Britain wishes to remain a parliamentary democracy. Power resides with the British people and is leased for a period of up to five years to a Parliament trusted to undertake open and free democratic debate. The electorate is then in a position to judge the actions of the majority and minority in that Parliament at a subsequent general election and to endorse them for a further period, or to change the balance in the way that they would like. British people have not consented to a big extension of judge-made law from the ECJ, nor have they openly voted for a system of administration and decision-making on crucial issues behind closed doors in Brussels under the influence of, and in response to the drafts of unelected Commissioners.

The first task must therefore be to restore British parliamentary democratic sovereignty in the name of the British people. To do this the legal structure for Britain needs to be clarified. The supremacy of Parliamentary law over ECJ decision-making can easily be reasserted with the agreement of our partners and the modification of the 1972 European Communities Act. We should remember that the EU on one definition of the current legal position only has legal powers in Britain because of that founding Act of Parliament and the treaty that underlies it. Countries can modify or change their views on treaties, and one Parliament can modify or change an Act of Parliament passed by another. If we accept that there has been an absolute change in our position with sovereignty passing from Parliament and statute and therefore the British people to ECJ decisions, and if we accept that treaties can never be modified or changed, then we have ceased to be a sovereign country.

The revised European Communities Act could also include a list of reserve powers where the UK people and Parliament will regard it as their right to make all of the important decisions. Remaining in the Community we would need to accept that certain areas of law like competition, trade, and commerce are carried out on a joint basis with our European partners, and we would need to accept that the European courts have to have some rights over these matters. Once we have made clear, again, that Parliament could overturn or veto in extremis, we then need to play fair and to show that it would not normally do this. Parliament should expect to have complete control in areas of considerable national importance like defence, foreign policy and taxation. Successive British governments have always said that they have preserved the veto on taxation matters. In practice, Britain's power to settle its own tax affairs has been subtly eroded over the years, especially in the fields of excise duties and VAT. The Commission and many of our partners are determined that this erosion should now become a landslide. They are desperate to raise more money on a Community-wide basis, and keen to deal with what they see as unfair tax competition in jurisdictions like the UK and the Republic of Ireland which keep their tax rates lower than elsewhere. The Community is determined to push through a savings or withholding tax, keen to push through a landfill tax and a climate levy, and to move on from there to impose higher overall rates of corporate taxation throughout the EU. The British Parliament and people need to preserve their right to independent taxation.

The British Parliament grew up through a series of bruising battles with the Crown over this very issue. It was the wish of those who paid the taxes to be represented in Parliament and to see some redress of their grievances that led to the massive extension of the English and of the British Parliament's powers from the Parliament of Simon de Montfort through the English Civil War. It was the same issue that led to the revolt of the American Colonies who felt it was unfair, being well educated in British constitutional practice, that they should be required to pay taxes levied by the British Crown and Parliament when they had no direct representation in that body.

These matters can be put right by an amended 1972 European Communities Act. Britain should say, as indeed the German constitution does, that the ultimate source of authority in the UK is not the ECJ but the United Kingdom Parliament. The Act should go on to say that Parliament has by treaty agreed to grant the ECJ powers in defined fields related to the single market we have joined and support. The Act should establish that in crucial areas like taxation, foreign policy, and big domestic policy areas like health and education, no power has been granted to the ECJ to interfere against our will.

The second thing British negotiators should seek to achieve in the renegotiation is a better deal in areas where the EU already has control and is the dominant shaping force. The sorest area for Britain in its 30-year membership of the EC so far has been the area of fishing. Settled almost as an afterthought in the original accession negotiations, the

British government gave away too much in allowing a common fisheries policy for the North Sea. It is one of the ironies of the situation that large fleets of Spanish trawlers may arrive in the North Sea to take our fish, but there is no similar common fishing policy in the Mediterranean allowing us to reciprocate. Indeed, the North Sea and the western approaches around Ireland and the west coast of Great Britain are the only maritime area subject to a common fishing policy at all. The Baltic, like the Mediterranean, is similarly free of any such encumbrance.

Fishing

The UK should seek to repatriate fishing matters. We should say that we want to harmonise the practices in the Mediterranean Sea, the Baltic Sea and the North Sea. We wish to have the same national control over our coastline and coastal waters as is enjoyed by Mediterranean countries. Whilst it is too late to save many of the great trawler fleets that have bitten the dust, particularly on the east coast of England and Scotland, it is possible to improve the position in the future. The UK should take its own view of what is a reasonable rate of extraction of fish from the sea in the interests of conservation, and could make sure that a bigger proportion of the permitted catch goes to British vessels rather than to foreign-flagged vessels. We would become the licensing and policy controlling authority. At the moment we have the rotten job of policing the policy without very much influence over drafting the policy itself.

Agriculture

The second area where Britain needs to gain a bigger say and more control is the area of agriculture. One of the disappointing features of the EU is that where it has almost total control, it has adopted a common policy which does great damage to the consumers, considerable damage to the poorer countries of the world, and yet still doesn't manage to keep the producers happy. The CAP burdens the average British family with an extra £20 per week on their food bill because it keeps prices well above world market levels. At the same time it combines this with a protectionist system which keeps out the cheaper product from many third world countries who would dearly love the opportunity to sell into the rich markets of Britain, France and Germany but are prevented by physical restrictions. Talk to any

British farmers about the CAP at the moment and, despite the high level of subsidy and protection, they do not have a good word to say about it. It is EU regulation that has helped wipe out most of the British beef industry through what is seen by farmers as a particularly heavy-handed response to BSE whilst failing to protect the health of people and animals. There is also a feeling that it was not an even-handed response, as British herds were not the only herds to be infected by BSE, but it was the UK that faced the full brunt of EU anger about the problems that had developed. Similarly, in the dairy sector, the UK was uniquely badly served by the original allocation of quotas. The quota system imposed by the EU means that British dairy farmers cannot expand their milk output even though their milk output is considerably below the amount of milk consumed in the UK. Other countries like France were given quota in excess of their domestic requirements.

A new system for agriculture would require careful construction. Whilst it should be possible to create a better regulatory framework for farmers in Britain by making more sensible decisions about milk output, beef herd control and similar issues, any new system of domestic subsidy to replace the current price control and EU subsidy system would need clearance through GATT to avoid another bruising trade row. Trade rows are common in GATT on agricultural matters. The World Trade Organization is understandably very critical both of the EU and the US for their complicated and expensive agricultural protection systems. The British government would have to enter discussions with the WTO, arguing that a domestic system of subsidy and protection would be less damaging than the EU one from which we were disengaging. It should be possible to reach an agreement, but it will require detailed analysis to satisfy the custodians of the GATT that our main aim in coming out of the CAP is not to increase the overall level of quota restriction, but to make a decisive shift in regulation in favour of British as opposed to continental farmers. Indeed, there may be allies and friends in the WTO who would see a Britain freed of most or all of the restrictions of CAP as a more useful ally in ensuing rounds of world trade talks designed to free the market in agricultural products more generally. Britain may well like to develop a system of agricultural support which concentrates on using the money freed from the breakup of the CAP to offer direct cash support to farmers whilst moving closer towards world pricing and a more open market in agricultural products.

The important thing is that in this area we would be out to assert more control and therefore more decision-making in Britain. There would be lively debate between consumer interests, in favour of a much more open market and lower prices, and producer interests in favour of protection geared to the specific interests of British farmers. Both groups would agree with any government move designed to halt the unfortunate intervention of EU policy-makers and administrators into the British farming scene, where the regulation both damages the customer whilst also favouring farmers outside the UK at the expense of those inside.

Overseas aid

A third area where the British government may like to renegotiate existing EU policies is in the area of overseas aid. It is this area which has attracted most criticism from within and without the Commission and the other European institutions. It was allegations of fraud and malpractice in the overseas aid budget that led directly to the downfall of the Commission in 1999 in general, and the Overseas Aid Commissioner, Madame Cresson, in particular. There is the general feeling that European aid is not well targeted, that the programmes are not well run, and that more audit work would reveal more irregularities. Overseas aid can be a very important part of building and supporting a foreign policy. As one of the aims of the renegotiation would be to make clear that Britain still intends to have an independent foreign policy, with a set of views that may be the same or may be different from our European partners on international issues, so it is important to back that up with the direct payment of more British money for good causes abroad which should be done at the expense of making such a big contribution through the EU.

Budget contribution

The final issue which needs to be resolved in the renegotiation is the issue of our budget contribution. As Britain has in mind participation in a common market rather than a common government, it is only fair that Britain should make a smaller financial contribution to the costs of running the whole than those partners who wish to create a United States of Europe and a strong central government in Brussels.

Margaret Thatcher attempted to resolve this dilemma in the 1980s. Her successful renegotiation then produced a British rebate which dealt with the immediate problems that our contribution was out of all proportion to our then wealth or our then involvement with the EEC. If we press ahead with repatriating fishing, parts of agriculture and overseas aid, we clearly need a new settlement on the budget. If we make clear that we wish to be members of the common market but not of the wider common government it is only reasonable that we should only make a contribution towards the common costs of running and policing that common market and not to the wider common costs of a growing bureaucratic European government. It is not possible to carry out the renegotiation without also looking at the question of the money.

The UK and the EU

Readers who believe that a stronger European government is inevitable and that Britain should go along with it will by now be saying to themselves that all these demands or requests from the UK are fanciful. They will argue that there is absolutely no way that they can be achieved in the real world. Similarly, my critics on the edges of the Eurosceptic coalition will be saying that none of these things can be achieved unless Britain threatens to withdraw. Would it not be better to withdraw to get rid of the many adverse features of the European Union as it is developing?, they will ask. We must now turn to what powers and pressures the UK could bring to bear in order to achieve some or all of these negotiating objectives.

The first thing to understand is that the UK has a wide-ranging weaponry in European discussion which it can deploy. It is a negotiation or a debate between member states. For those who wish to see it as warfare by another means, the analogy would be that withdrawal from the Community is the nuclear weapon, whereas there are many other conventional weapons that could be deployed to good effect. Since 1945, the UK and the US have unfortunately regularly had to take up arms to settle a number of major and minor problems around the world. Never once have these two nuclear powers used their nuclear weapons, as they understand that the point of a nuclear weapon is to act as a deterrent.

So it would be with these negotiations to keep us in a common market. The first conventional weapon that the UK has at its disposal is the veto on any further treaty changes. Under the constitutional framework of the EU, it requires the consent of every member state before any change can be made in the founding treaties. The French and German governments and the Commission are well known to want substantial further changes to the treaties beyond the changes proposed at Nice. All of these changes will still require the consent of the British government. The French and German governments wish to press on with an inner core of countries to much deeper entanglement in a European government. Again, this procedure requires the consent of the UK.

Britain can therefore say in any treaty negotiation that it is not prepared to allow the others to go ahead in the way they wish unless its legitimate concerns are also taken into account. We should not agree to any single treaty modification, however desirable or undesirable, unless and until our requests for a different constitutional settlement for ourselves are taken seriously and moves are made to accommodate them.

The second power we have is the power to delay or impede existing business of the Union under the existing treaties. British parliamentarians are well used to the daily guerrilla warfare in the House of Commons. One of the main weapons the Opposition has at its disposal in Parliament is the weapon of time. Legitimate scrutiny, sensible questions, lengthy but relevant debate, are all tried and tested ways of delaying the government of the day. Scope for doing this in the EU is considerably greater. Many of the other players in the game are not used to British parliamentary tactics or ways. Given the large corpus of treaty law, ECJ judgments and procedural precedents, it is quite possible to delay business for very lengthy periods by astute coalition-building, by use of the rather ramshackle procedures of the EU, and by constant recourse to the courts where necessary. As the EU lives by the law courts, so it could be made to suffer by those same courts.

The third weapon at Britain's command is the weapon of money. Britain is the second largest net contributor to the EU. The cheques Britain sends on a regular basis are substantial and are important to paying the wage bills of officials in Brussels as well as paying for the expensive programmes of agriculture, overseas aid and regional aid that the Commission disburses. If the EU is totally unwilling to cooperate by examining Britain's agenda for a different kind of relationship to some of the others, then Britain could start to query why it is paying so much and could easily find legal reasons related to the lack of performance, fraud or incompetent administration of programmes in the EU as to why Britain should go slow or hold up payments to the Commission.

I am not recommending that we should do any of these things. Indeed, I think it is quite obvious that Britain would not have to behave like this as soon as it showed considerable political will in wishing to have a renegotiation. An honest British prime minister should go to Brussels immediately after winning an election on a platform of renegotiation and explain our position.

That British prime minister should say that we are sorry that there has been such a wide range of misunderstandings between successive UK governments and our partners over many years. We should say that British politicians have consistently told the British people that we are joining a common market where we can also make progress on some other common policies on areas like environment and transport where it makes sense for us as well as for them. British politicians have never set out, in the way that French and German politicians have set out, the full vision of a properly integrated federal or centralised Europe. Because the British people have not been readied for this and have not been persuaded that they want in, we are now in the position where many British people wish to be in the trading arrangements but do not wish to proceed towards political, monetary and judicial union. The British prime minister should say that the fault is probably more that of Britain than of our partners. No one can deny that our partners have in recent years been crystal clear about what they are trying to achieve. It has been the wrong-headedness of British politicians who have wished to keep their heads in the sand over the true intentions of our partners because they know the British people will not go along with them that has done more of the damage, rather than the attitudes of our partners themselves.

The British prime minister should continue by saying that the British people genuinely want to make a success of the common market we joined and we believe we still have a lot to offer when it comes to helping fashion a policy of low tariffs, less regulation, less intervention and common business law codes across the Community. We wish to remain full members of the single market and wish to contribute to its development. We would be quite happy to attend other meetings on other subjects as a country with a veto to see if we can reach agreement with our partners on items of foreign policy, social policy, whatever. What we cannot do is accept an ever-tightening, more centralised Community with less and less control over what happens in Britain as a result.

The prime minister should continue by saying that we are quite happy to continue making a financial contribution towards the administration and success of the single market. We accept that we will be net contributors, but we believe that our contribution should be related to the number of policy areas that we wish to be designed and policed from Brussels. Clearly, our net contribution per head should be lower than that of Germany or France, who wish to have a much bigger government of Western Europe.

In return for granting Britain membership of the common market but not of the common government, the UK would then remove any remaining obstacles in the way of all those who wish Europe to proceed at whatever pace they choose towards a more heavily integrated system. We will not be joining the Euro, but we wish it every success. As a big trading partner just offshore from Euroland and as one of the big financial markets of the world, we wish to see the Euro's success and we will take any domestic action that Euroland would like and we agree is necessary in order to help create the conditions for the stability and success for the Euro. Similarly, if France and Germany wish to proceed rapidly as they seem to do with creating a common army, navy and air force, we would be very happy to work alongside that defence force through NATO when we have common cause. However, we would not wish to commit our own forces to a separate European defence force that operated outside the framework of NATO, and we would certainly not wish to commit our forces to any military adventure which did not have the consent of the British people and government.

If Britain were allowed a relationship that made most of the people in Britain feel much happier, then many of the continuing running sores would go away. Britain would be kept advised of what the EU was trying to do next in all the areas that were reserved to the UK Parliament, and Britain could volunteer to join in whenever it saw fit.

We might find that Britain wanted to join in with rather more than has been the case to date where there has been an element of coercion through qualified majority voting, legal actions and Commission pressure. The problem of the UK has not been settled for some forty years. In the 1950s, the UK itself was rather dismissive of the *Club des Battus* forming on the continent and decided it wasn't going to be significant. In the 1960s, the UK changed its view, only to be met with resistance from De Gaulle, who rightly perceived that the UK would be a destabilising influence on what he saw even in those faraway days as an emerging European Union. In the 1970s, Britain was admitted to the club, only to find that from the day of its admission onwards, it was always being asked to deliver rather more to the central power of Brussels than it wished. Early rows under Labour and the Conservatives over the financial contribution were soon replaced by endless rows over how much power the Brussels government should have, and how many more things were going to be transferred from British parliamentary control to EU bureaucratic decision.

The UK has to gain confidence in its own position. There is a tug of love and hate in Britain about the EU itself. Whilst a big majority of people do not want more government from Brussels, and are certainly against Brussels taxation, the single currency, and the idea of sending our troops into a war where we have lost the vote, there is also a mood amongst the majority that we do not wish to be thrown out, we do not wish to take our bat away completely, and we do need to trade with our partners and be friends with them wherever possible. It is this mood which would be captured by the renegotiation set out above. Of course, there will be critics who say that none of this can be achieved and that our partners would not wish Britain to have the benefits of trade in the common market without more of the costs and problems of the common government. This attitude takes a very mean-minded approach to our European partners, and it also implies that all the other things they are trying to do are unhelpful, which is even more reason why we should not be involved with them. To those who say that by narrowing our interests to the single or common market we are doing ourselves a disfavour, the answer is easy. Under the model I have sketched any British government could opt into any part of what the EU was doing at any time, and I am sure this would be welcomed. Our partners would clearly like us to agree with them more often than we do at present. But what we would have achieved by the renegotiation is the preservation of the ultimate power of the British people and, through them, their Parliament to change our minds over individual policies and areas when we see fit. Britain is a country that does not like being coerced. If we are left free to do things we may be more agreeable partners.

France and Germany have a lot to gain from this proposal. They must be heartily sick of the UK problem. Every time they wish to develop their club in the way they have set out, they find that they have Britain trying to organise the awkward squad in the EU to slow them down or prevent them. Germany wants to stop its citizens putting deposits in Luxembourg and escaping German tax. Without British intervention Germany may have been able to use the EU institutions to impose a withholding tax as it favours. With Britain's intervention, so far this has proved impossible. Of course, there would be haggling over what was a fair contribution to reflect those parts of the EU we wish to join, but we would be building on the variable geometry European approach which is emerging as the norm. We already have different types of member of the EU.

The neutral countries in the EU have made clear they want no part of the emerging defence policy. Greece and the UK have opted out of the common frontiers, or the Schengen Agreement, because Greece and the main island of the UK do not have common land borders with the other members of the Community. Three countries including the UK have opted out of the single currency so far. And France has from time to time opted out of NATO, which was been the most effective means of defending Western Europe in the post-war period.

Britain does not, however, want a two-speed Europe. The idea of a two-speed Europe implies that we are all going to the same place, it's just that some of us are dilatory about getting there. Looking at the lack of success of British foreign policy in general and the Eurocentric foreign policy in particular in the post-war period, I can see why many of the critics of Britain do see the issue in terms of two-speed rather than variable geometry. In all previous cases where Britain has offered dogged resistance to a set of policies for months or even years, Britain has usually caved in in the end. Britain tried to get a better deal on fishing before joining the Community, but gave in in order to complete the session negotiations. Britain has long said that it wants a reformed CAP but it has never managed to pull it off. Britain said for many years that it wanted nothing to do with the Social Chapter, but has now, under a different government, signed up to it. Britain made clear that it needed an opt-out from the single currency because it had many doubts and problems with it, but now has a government which says in principle they wish to join it when the conditions are right. The expectation on the continent is always that a reluctant Britain will be dragged kicking and screaming, but will eventually end up at the same destination as the rest.

This is why we need a new British government which will clearly set out the mood of the British people and get our partners to understand that we are serious in saying we want a different kind of friendly relationship with them from those of the core countries who wish to complete a political, economic and monetary union. It will take time to persuade them of the seriousness of this point, but any EU witness of the present British debate must begin to see that this is the way the mood of the British people is developing. If the EU and the Commission wish to see more favourable press about themselves in our tabloid newspapers, they should understand that the best way of achieving this is to admit a renegotiation along the lines outlined above.

Some in this debate believe that the only real answer is for Britain to pull out of the EU altogether. This is not the view of the Conservative Party and, judging by recent polls and opinion surveys, it is not the majority view of the British people. However, now that some 40 per cent of the British people regularly tell pollsters that they themselves would like to pull out of the EU altogether, it is worth examining what the consequences of this would be and how it would differ from renegotiation.

The first thing to understand is that it is different from renegotiation. It would be perceived as very different by political opponents in Britain and it would be seen as very different by EU partners. This would be for the very simple reason that it is a different policy. Withdrawal from the EU means that Britain has decided categorically and for the foreseeable future that there is no way that Britain can gain anything from belonging to the EU and that life would be better outside it altogether. Where the approach of renegotiation is based upon a certain honesty and humility with our partners, offering them solutions to the British problem that has bedevilled them for so long, withdrawal is an action designed to anger them and to make it more difficult to develop satisfactory relationships with them once withdrawal has taken place.

Withdrawal from the EU is perfectly feasible for the simple reason that the EU does not yet have a standing army or standing police force in Britain to prevent us taking charge of our own affairs again. Indeed, there is a clear precedent for withdrawal from the EU in English history. The Reformation took place by decision of the executive government, in this case the king, endorsed by a series of parliamentary statutes. It was a unilateral action carried out against the wishes of the papal authorities who had legal jurisdiction and power in Britain but who had no standing army or police force in the country to enforce their powers. The crucial statute, the Statute of Appeals in 1533, asserted British sovereignty and struck away with a flourish of the legislative pen all papal legal jurisdiction in England and Wales. It led on to sweeping changes in English and Welsh society with a massive transfer of property represented by the dissolution of the monasteries, the pillaging of churches, the re-education of the clergy and the assertion of the king's control over all ecclesiastical matters as the supreme head and governor of the Church.

The reaction of our European friends and allies to this was, not surprisingly, one of considerable anger. Catholic powers, who were the dominant powers on the continent at the time, threatened Britain in all sorts of ways. The full moral and political wrath of the papacy was hurled down on England and there were threats of foreign armies backing up the assertion of papal power. The row was still going on as late as 1588, when the Spanish Armada arrived, a potent force designed to reassert Catholic authority and the supremacy of the Pope in England some 55 years after the crucial statute had removed all vestiges of papal power from these shores. It was only the defeat of the Armada and the subsequent successful pursuit of the Spanish War that confirmed England's right to self-determination.

No one is suggesting that withdrawal from the EU would result in a similar attempt by the continental forces to reassert control in Britain by military means. However, in EU terms, unilateral withdrawal of Britain and renunciation of the treaty would be a hostile and an illegal act. The EU might try to assert by legal means its rights to jurisdiction over the UK, but this would undoubtedly peter out, given their predicted unwillingness to back up the legal requests with any force. The important point about all this is that relationships would have been damaged by unscripted and unilateral withdrawal and it might take some time to rebuild friendships and alliances after such a big event. We could not expect any cooperation by our European partners as we tried to disentangle all the many things that have been muddled up with the continent as a result of our almost thirty years' membership of the EU to date. We have to accept that a lot of our law codes, especially in the areas of competition, business and industrial policy, have been built in common with our European partners. We have to accept that the European court system is part of the enforcement mechanism, and the words of the treaty are important in the way businesses conduct themselves in the UK as well as on the continent. Those advocating withdrawal would have to decide how much they wished to keep and how much of it would need revisiting or reasserting once the European court and legal system had been swept aside from the UK. As far as I can see all of it would need re-basing in British statute law and businesses would need reassuring that the important parts of the law codes would remain in place and would remain compatible with those on the continent.

Advocates of immediate withdrawal point out that there would be many offsetting benefits. It is clearly true that if we withdrew unilaterally from the Community tomorrow, we would save a lot of money. The £10 000 million gross contribution we make to the Community would no longer be payable. We would be able to decide how much of that we wished to spend on agriculture, regional aid and overseas aid, the principal uses of the funds through the EU, and how much of it we wished to give back to taxpayers by means of a tax cut or rebate. It is also true that as the EU countries sell us more than we sell them, it is difficult to believe that they would seek a trade confrontation by imposing penal tariffs upon our exports. They would get into immediate difficulties with the World Trade Organization if they did, and they would be vulnerable to retaliation.

The more likely worry of businesses and many people who do not advocate immediate withdrawal is the subtle pressures that could be exerted. Our experiences with the British beef crisis have shown what an impact bad relations can have on trade. Because relations between Britain, on the one hand, and France in particular, on the other, were inflamed through the EU, French customers boycotted English products and French farmers took retaliatory illegal action against

British farm products on the move through France. If Britain handles its relationships with the EU clumsily, it could have a further impact on unfavourable consumer attitudes towards various British products. More importantly, if we had alienated the administrations of France and Germany more than we have done so far by our dilatory and unhelpful EU policy, it would be quite possible for those jurisdictions to produce bureaucratic obstacles to a fair and free trade, as they have done during the period of our membership.

Those who favour withdrawal can say that it is a more honest policy than the one that we have at the moment. It would clearly signal the growing impatience of many in Britain with decisions coming from the EU and with the intentions of the EU's founders. It would save us a lot of money, and it would send a clear message to British business that the world is our oyster, not just the European market. The Labour and Liberal parties, the Confederation of British Industry and others would be implacably opposed. Handled badly, it would make a damaging impact upon our relations with the leading continental countries and it would give many British people a feeling that they had burned their boats and were rather isolated. Because the British people voted so conclusively in 1975 to stay in a common market, I think it preferable that a new British prime minister open friendly but clear negotiations with our European partners to produce a new kind of relationship that makes sense for us and them, rather than announcing a unilateral intention to withdraw at a specified date.

One of the advantages about developing a new relationship is that it enables us to think globally rather than in narrower European terms. Many of the problems confronting European government in the business area are better solved on a global basis. The EU is working out mezzanine regulation of banking, financial services, telecommunications, transport and the like. Yet all of these things should now be looked at globally. If there are to be transnational standards for telecommunications, if there is to be transnational law on intercepting messages and cracking fraud, if there is to be transnational regulation to ensure honest bank deposits or successful international flights, this should be done on a worldwide basis by the consent of the important countries involved, rather than by creating an unnecessary regional set of regulations on top of the national ones and the evolving global ones. Britain's new settlement with Europe would enable us to be in the vanguard with the US, Japan and others in negotiating these global standards which could drive forward the emerging global market.

The alternative European vision

A minority of people in Britain do think that France and Germany are right. They believe that the EU has made a singular contribution to the development of post-war Europe. They believe that in some mysterious way the EU has been the creator of peace and prosperity. Those of us who disagree say that the peace has been kept in Western Europe by the massive presence of US firepower and by the creation of stable democracies in Western Europe who no longer wish to fight each other. Prosperity has come about through successive GATT rounds, now under the guidance of the World Trade Organization, and by the development of a sophisticated global trading pattern which has enabled more and more national and local specialisation.

Nonetheless, it is a sincerely held view that European integration is good for Europe, it is inevitable, it is strongly wanted by our partners and therefore we should go along with it. It is therefore important to ask ourselves what would the world look like if we did accept that France and Germany were right and willingly joined in their schemes.

Were we to do so, we would first of all have to make an important creative leap. We would have to accept that whilst we would remain British linguistically and culturally, we would become citizens of the new Europe and should look to the European institutions for government, for foreign and economic policy and for general guidance. We should transfer our political loyalties to the EU whilst keeping our cultural loyalties closer to home. The UK is to a united EU as Wales is to the UK. Our national songs, sports teams and language would be no less powerfully supported because we had accepted government from a more distant capital, but we would have to accept that we were no longer a self-governing, independent democracy.

Britain might be able to make an important contribution to the development of such a United States of Europe. The obvious thing for

Britain to do would be to say that one of the most disagreeable features of the way in which the EU is emerging is the concentration of power in the hands of unelected Commissioners and, to a lesser extent, in the hands of secretive Ministers from national parliaments. If we truly wanted to be part of the great European project, it should be Britain that took upon itself the task of turning the European Parliament into a proper parliament, with powers to tax and to legislate. The government of Europe should emerge from that parliament and that government should be tried and tested through all the usual opposition guiles. Of course, it would require transnational parties, campaigning on transnational tickets and the creation of a whole series of issues which were seen as European issues rather than national issues handled in Brussels. The Commission would have to be scaled back to an active civil service, and the front men and women would have to emerge from the elected in the parliament itself. This would create a more democratic culture than we currently see in the emerging EU and would deal with some of the problems that people have identified in terms of lack of accountability and the democratic deficit.

Britain might be surprised to find that it could actually influence some of that, if at the same time it wanted to create a powerful state based around such a parliament with its own armies, currency, court system, legal codes and control of business. In the absence of any British leadership the terms available for British entry into the system are not good. We would become a province of the new European empire. We would be an important part of it, making a substantial contribution from our taxes to support the central government, but, as life has shown in recent years, we would have very little influence over what the government of that super-state did. On the current model our voice would be reduced, losing at least one Commissioner, and losing a proportion of our MEPs. The course is fully set out already by the French and German governments, and Britain is rather late to the game in trying to influence it. For my own part, I do not think it can work as I do not believe that the peoples of Western Europe are ready for such a revolution yet. Europe is designed to remain a bickering Tower of Babel, not a uniform and purposeful single country. There are no advantages for Britain in joining the present Franco-German scheme for a bigger government in Brussels.

I doubt if we could make the EU genuinely democratic – we have left it too late. I do not think a country with so many languages, different histories and interests could come together and be at peace with itself. It is better not to try than to bring about decades of unrest and unease over the project itself. We do not want a United Europe full of Basque and Irish struggles against the central power.

9
Conclusions

The new world of the web, of global capital, of footloose businesses and of rapid technical change is teeming with opportunity. It is also making the old political ideas look rather dated. This book has shown how the new technology will drive changes in the way we work, shop and play. The relentless movement to a global market is giving ever more scope to the English-speaking world to sell its computers, its information, its culture and its entertainment. It is making national government solutions irrelevant or unhelpful, as the pace of change outstrips the capacity of individual governments to keep up.

In this fast-moving world, people are seeking certainty in older faiths and associations. The old nations of Europe retain loyalty. Newer countries often split under the pressures as people assert their preference for an older smaller area and political system. Whilst many see the need for more global government and regulation, even in the US which would have most influence on the process, there is a scepticism about how desirable this is.

This book has demonstrated that the mighty project to create a United States of Europe is proceeding apace, but is unlikely to make the world a safer or better place. Instead, it is likely to lead to a trial of strength between two cultural and governing systems: the US democratic free trade one, and the Europe bureaucratic and regulated one. The 1950s and 1960s were dominated by a conflict between the communist and capitalist models, which was finally won without a shot being fired in anger between the two main protagonists, the US and the USSR, when the Western model proved so much more capable of delivering economic success. The next 20 years are likely to be dominated by a contest between the Europeans who think that governments can make societies better, and the North Americans who think free enterprise makes a bigger contribution to health and riches.

The beginnings of the conflict are there for all to see, in the escalating trade disputes and the outlines of a row over independent European forces and foreign policy. US policy-makers will have to pull back from their enthusiasm for this emerging super-state and take stock of their position. They will find that what they may gain in a simpler command structure in Europe as one government displaces many, they will lose in terms of influence and friendship as that government sets out to rival the US.

The US is keen to expand its influence and the geographical reach of its ideas by expanding NAFTA. Several South American countries are likely to be early entrants, following Mexico. The US sees it as a way of spreading the ideas of limited government, light regulation, lower taxes and free trade on a broader front. UK membership would make a dramatic difference to the way the US and the EU are shaping up. If the old special relationship could be brought up to date by British membership of the latest American club, the balance of Western debate would shift more in favour of free trade and enterprise away from bigger government.

We have seen how the UK and the US have worked together in the post-war world to create peace and stability, to defend threatened smaller nations and to advance the cause of democracy worldwide. The book sets out why it makes more sense to strengthen these ties for both sides than for the UK to become an important region in the new European state. Some US commentators ask, 'Why can't Britain be like Texas in the US union and accept the Euro just as Texas accepts the dollar?' The answer is simple. Britain is not playing Texas to Germany's California. The correct analogy is between the national members of NAFTA and the position of Britain in Europe. No one in the US thinks that the US should surrender its dollar to join a new single currency system with Mexico and Canada, so why should Britain do that on the other side of the Atlantic?

The institutions that made up the post-1945 settlement are by and large still capable of adaptation to the emerging new conditions. Institutions like the Commonwealth are flexible, not too intrusive.

They come together when there is a problem or a purpose. The World Trade Organization makes good progress in spreading free trade ever more widely. It is organisations that try to become alternative governments that threaten the spirit of the age, and threaten to burden participating countries beyond their patience.

The size and power of the new United States of Europe is quite considerable, but it is lop-sided. It has a powerful potential army, but lacks capacity to operate beyond its own continent. It would be better if the European countries remained faithful members of NATO and the UN, not complicating matters by creating a new level of military organisation and bureaucracy. The economic strength is considerable, but the economies of the continent are inward-looking and the forces of protectionism are latent. The EU begins to look like an old organisation, developed from ideas that are now 50 years out of date. It is born of an era where coal and steel were the crucial industries, where agriculture was the dominant activity and where keeping France and Germany together was the most important issue. Today the problems are very different. There is no likelihood of modern Germany invading France, but a very cumbersome structure has been established just in case.

The book shows that the US has plenty of options, but should be careful about the EU. It also shows that the UK has plenty of choices, but needs to make up its mind soon on which way it is to go. The UK's decision on how much European integration to accept is awaited with baited breath on the continent of Europe. It should also be of great interest to Washington. If the UK chooses more freedom and democracy, it will mean a stronger transatlantic alliance and give a great boost to the forces of freedom everywhere. If the UK chooses further continental entanglements, it will be a dark day for freedom and free trade and will usher in a long period of international tension. Two systems will have to battle it out, with much more even forces on both sides. It will make for many conflicts, as European peoples wrestle against the new imperial power from within and the US comes to terms with it from without.

Notes

Introduction

The progress of the debate about British membership of the EEC can be charted in the *Hansard* record of parliamentary debates. The government set out its thinking on 7 July 1971, Hansard cols 1338–1341 in the Statement on the White Paper about membership, and again on 28 October 1971, cols 2197–2212.

The Union of England with Wales under the Tudors is covered in Elton (1997), especially pp. 175–7; and the union with Scotland in Ashley (1965), pp. 228–31.

The policy of the Labour government on devolution is set out in Redwood (1999).

Writing is only just catching up with the breathless dot.com phenomenon. I found Davis and Meyer (1998) captured the mood well.

Chapter 1

Sampson (1965) (1982) sets out the institutional structure of the UK.

Walker (1970) gives an insider's view of the workings of government.

Bogdanor (1999) provides a Liberal view of the changes to government structure in the UK in recent years.

Jenkins (1995) attacks the centralisation of power in quangos under the Conservatives, a process which has got far worse since 1997.

The views of other commentators on the present trends in British politics and society can be read in Hitchens (1999), Heffer (1999), and Marr (1999).

The new style of European history is typified by the blockbuster work of Norman Davies (Davies 1996).

The wider themes of nationhood and ethnicity are well studied in Mortimer (1999).

Chapter 2

The two important speeches by Sir Winston Churchill are 'The Sinews of Peace', Fulton, Missouri, 5 March 1946, and 'The Tragedy of Europe', Zurich, 19 September 1946.

Chancellor Kohl's thoughts are set out in 'Our Future in Europe', Edinburgh, 23 May 1991, 'The European Process is Irreversible', Munich, May 1992, and 'Speech on Receiving the Honorary Freedom of the City of London', 18 February 1998.

Jacques Chirac spoke in Berlin on 27 June 2000 in a speech called 'Our Europe'.

Churchill's four-volume *History of the English-Speaking Peoples* (Cassell, 1957) is useful here and for other parts of the historical narrative.

Chapter 3

Nye and Morpurgo (1955) chart the way in which the US rebelled against the mother country and came of age.

The Fontana History of Europe examines Franco-British rivalry, especially in Rude (1965) and Grenville (1976).

Bullock's (1952) work remains a classic study of the racist and imperialist ambitions of German Nazism.

Chapter 4

The Agreement establishing the World Trade Organization is a long and complex document. There are annexes delaing with Intellectual Property, settlement of disputes, trade policy, government procurement and a series of sector agreements.

The founding agreement of the IMF was first drawn up in 1945 at a UN Monetary and Financial Conference.

The International Bank for Reconstruction and Development *Articles of Agreement*, 16 February 1989.

The Commonwealth's evolution can be traced through *The Declaration of Principles*, Singapore, 1971; *The Lusaka Declaration*, Zambia, 1979; *The Harare Commonwealth Declaration*, Zimbabwe, 1991; and *The Millbank Action Programme*, New Zealand, 1995.

These are all reproduced in the *Commonwealth Year Book* for 1998.

Bayne (1997), Howell (1998) and Marshall (1998) provide good articles on the Commonwealth.

NATO was established under *The North Atlantic Treaty*, Washington, DC, 4 April 1949.

Chapter 5

The shifting patterns of world trade in favour of the English-speaking world are reported in *Eurofacts* A Global Britain publication, 14 July 2000.

The impact of the US on the continent of Europe is illuminated in Lindemann (1995).

The North American Free Trade Agreement: *Eurofacts*, 10 September 1999, 'How to lose market share', charts how NAFTA's share of world trade has risen and the EU's has fallen, 1987–97.

Jamieson and Minford (1999) make a good statistical comparison between the US and the EU on trade, taxes and jobs.

Chapter 6

Eurofacts, Global Britain (1999) sets out the main figures on Britain's pattern of trade with EU and NAFTA countries.

British Management Data Foundation charts the progress of the two currencies.

The early claims for the Euro from 1 January 2000 onwards were detailed in the *Financial Times* during January 2000.

Chapter 7

Thomson (1972) gives a view of twentieth-century UK foreign policy.

Clark (1998) offers a distinctive historical view, being especially interesting on the military history of the period.

Chapter 8

Any study of the UK's relationship with the EU should begin with HMSO (1970); the Prime Minister's speech recommending membership, 28 October 1971, *Hansard*, cols 2197–2212; and *European Communities White Paper*, July 1971, London.

The European Central Bank has set out its views on the new Euro currency in Duisenberg (1999).

The British government discusses the draft Treaty of Nice in *IGC: Reform for Enlargement* (2000).

Howe (1999) examines the issues which would need to be negotiated with the EU partners.

Brussels' ambitions to tax member states were set out in *Towards Tax Co-ordination in the European Union: A Package to Tackle Harmful Tax Competition*, Brussels, 1 October 1997.

The UK business case against more European integration is recorded in European Research Group (1998).

The background on the evolution of Europe is traced in Hill (1993), Booker and North (1994), Jamieson (1994), Hilton (1997) and Stevens (1997).

Leach (1999) is a good beginner's guide to the institutions viewed from a sceptical vantage point.

Bibliography

Ashley, M. (1965) *England in the Seventeenth Century*. London: Penguin.

Bayne, N. (1997) 'Globalization and the Commonwealth', *The Round Table*, vol. 344.

Bogdanor, V. (1999) *Devolution in the United Kingdom*. Oxford: Oxford University Press.

Booker, C. and North, R. (1994) *The Mad Officials*. London: Constable.

British Management Data Foundation (1999) *Currency Volatility: The Steadiness of the £ sterling against the US Dollar*. Sheepscombe, Gloucestershire: BMDF.

Bullock, A. (1952) *Hitler: A Study in Tyranny*. London: Penguin.

Chirac, J. (2000) 'Our Europe'. Speech at Berlin, 27 June.

Churchill, W. (1946) 'The Sinews of Peace'. Speech at Fulton, Missouri, 5 March.

Churchill, W. (1946) 'The Tragedy of Europe'. Speech at Zurich, 19 September.

Churchill, W. (1957) *History of the English Speaking Peoples*. London: Cassell.

Clark, A. (1998) *The Tories: Conservatives and the Nation State*. London: Weidenfeld and Nicolson.

Commonwealth Yearbook (1998) *The Declaration of Principles,* Singapore, 1971; *The Lusaka Declaration,* Zambia, 1979; *The Harare Commonwealth Declaration,* Zimbabwe, 1991; *The Millbank Action Programme,* New Zealand, 1995.

Connolly, B. (1995) *The Rotten Heart of Europe*, London: Faber and Faber.

Davies, N. (1996) *Europe: A History*. Oxford: Oxford University Press.

Davis, S. and Meyer, C. (eds) (1998) *Blur*. Oxford: Capstone

Duisenberg, W. (1999) 'A Stable Euro', *European Quarterly*, Autumn.

Elton, G.R. (1997) *England Under the Tudors*. London: Folio Society.

Eurofacts (1999) Global Britain, 'How to Lose Market Share', 10 September. London.

Eurofacts (1999) *UK Trade in 1998 and Growth 1992–1998,* London.

Eurofacts (2000) Reports on shifting patterns of world trade in favour of the English-speaking world, 14 July, London.

European Research Group (1998) *Business Agenda for a Free Europe*. London: ERG (March).

Financial Times. Early claims for the Euro, January 2000.

Foreign Office (2000) *IGC: Reform for Enlargement*. London, February.

Global Britain (1999) *UK Trade in 1998 and Growth 1992–1998*. London.

Gordon Walker, P. (1970) *The Cabinet*. London: Fontana.

Grenville, J.A.S. (1976) *Europe Reshaped 1848–1878*, Fontana History of Europe. London: Fontana.

European Communities White Paper, July 1971.

Hansard, Official Report of Parliamentary debates, 7 July 1971, cols 1338–1341; 28 October 1971, cols 2197–2212.

HMSO (1970) *Britain and the European Communities: An Economic Assessment*. London: HMSO.

Heffer, S. (1999) *Nor Shall My Sword*. London: Weidenfeld and Nicolson.
Hill, S. (ed.) (1997), *Visions of Europe*. London: Gerald Duckworth.
Hilton, A. (1997) *The Principality and Power of Europe*. Herts: Dorchester House.
Hitchens, P. (1999) *The Abolition of Britain*. London: Quartet Books.
House of Commons Foreign Affairs Select Committee *The Future Role of the Commonwealth* House of Commons Paper 45, 1995–6 Session.
Howe, M. (1999) *Could the UK Join a Global Free Trade Association?* London: IEA.
Howell, D. (1998) 'The Place of the Commonwealth in the International Order', *The Round Table*, vol. 345.
IBRD (1989) *Articles of Agreement*, 16 February.
IMF (1945) Founding Agreement. Bretton Woods: IMF.
Jamieson, B. (1994) *Britain beyond Europe*. London: Gerald Duckworth.
Jamieson, B. and Minford, P. (1999) *Britain and Europe: Choices for Change*. London: Politico.
Jenkins, S. (1995) *Accountable to None*. London: Hamish Hamilton.
Kohl, H. (1991) 'Our Future in Europe'. Speech at Edinburgh, 23 May.
Kohl, H. (1992) 'The European Process in Irreversible'. Speech at Munich, May.
Kohl, H. (1998) 'Speech on Receiving the Honorary Freedom of the City of London'. 18 February.
Leach, R. (1998) *Europe: A Concise Encyclopaedia*. London: Profile Books.
Lindemann, B. (ed.) (1995) *America Within Us*. Mainz: Hase and Koehler Verlag.
Marr, A. (2000) *The Day Britain Died*. London: Profile Books.
Marshall, P. (1998) 'The United Kingdom, the Commonwealth and the EU', *The Round Table*, vol. 347.
Mortimer, E. (ed.) (1999) *People, Nations and State: The Meaning of Ethnicity and Nationalism*. London: I.B. Tauris.
NATO (1949) *The North Atlantic Treaty*, Washington, DC, 4 April.
Nye, R.B. and Morpurgo, J.E. (1955) *A History of the United States*. London: Penguin.
Official Journal of the European Communities 30.6.2000 Decision No. 2/2000 of the EC–Mexico Joint Council of 23 March 2000 (the EU/Mexico Trade Agreement).
Redwood, J. (1999) *The Death of Britain?* Basingstoke: Macmillan.
Rude, G. (1965) *Revolutionary Europe 1783–1815*, Fontana History of Europe. London: Fontana.
Sampson, A. (1965) *Anatomy of Britain*. London: Hodder and Stoughton.
Sampson, A. (1982) *The Changing Anatomy of Britain*. London: Hodder and Stoughton.
Stevens, R. (1997) *About Europe*. London: Bluebell Press.
Thomson, D. (1972) *Europe since Napoleon*. London: Penguin.
Towards Tax Co-ordination in the European Union: A Package to Tackle Harmful Tax Competition. Brussels, 1 October 1997.
van Buitenen, P. (2000) *Blowing the Whistle*. London: Politico.
World Trade Organization, Agreement establishing the World Trade Organization. Marrakesh, 15 April 1994.

Index